WILD LONE

D J Watkins-Pitchford 'BB'

More often he had the scented tree aisles to himself

WILD LONE

The Story of a Pytchley Fox

Written and Illustrated by
D. J. WATKINS-PITCHFORD
('B.B.')

METHUEN & CO LTD
in association with
EYRE & SPOTTISWOODE LTD
11 NEW FETTER LANE, LONDON EC4

Also by 'B.B.'
MANKA, THE SKY GIPSY
The story of a Wild Goose
THE LITTLE GREY MEN
DOWN THE BRIGHT STREAM

First published in Great Britain
1939 by Eyre & Spottiswoode
Second edition 1951
New edition 1970
Text and illustrations copyright 1939 by D. J. Watkins-Pitchford
Printed in Great Britain by The Redwood Press Ltd,
Trowbridge & London
SBN 416 14590 6

To Sheila Ashley
This book is dedicated

"The wonder of the world, the beauty and the power, the shapes of things, their colours, lights, and shades; these I saw. Look ye also while life lasts."

FOREWORD

IT is thirty-one years since *Wild Lone* was first published—a lifetime! Ever since, there has been a steady demand for it, both from hunting people and naturalists. I must confess that this has been a continual source of astonishment to me.

As a general rule, the life history of an animal has a limited appeal, unless we can produce a masterpiece such as Williamson's *Tarka the Otter*. Perhaps the reason lies in the fact that the story is something more than the life history of a wild animal. When I wrote it I seemed to be possessed by some tremendous driving urge to put down all I knew of the midland countryside at all seasons of the year, the secret scents and sounds of the fields and spinneys, and great oak woodlands of Northamptonshire, where I wandered as a boy.

At the time I wrote this story, I was teaching at Rugby School and after the day's work I would come home and write far into the small hours of the morning. I could not write fast enough, the tedious effort of forming the written words seemed agonizingly slow. I wrote until I was exhausted and my hand was cramped; even then, the story was bursting to unfold.

Maybe other writers have had this truly wonderful experience. There was something mysterious, almost mystical about it, as though some power outside myself was taking over.

And how I looked forward to each evening when I could sit down at my table by the light of an oil lamp in that little panelled room and feel the magic working in me in the old quiet house!

When I described Rufus the fox setting out on his evening's hunting I seemed to become a fox! The mysterious moonlit ridings, the sombre thickets, the rustle of mice, and the calling of the birds of the night were amazingly vivid, as were the first, far off sinister sounds of the Hunt, drawing steadily nearer on the cold and misty winter air.

Each trackway, copse, and wood I knew, each field and hedgerow about my home, which was but a mile or so from the Pytchley kennels.

Many of these woods and gorse covers, famous finds for the Pytchley Hunt over a quarter of a century ago, have gone, so have the copses and hedgerows. Coldhangar, and the dark wood pool have vanished, the pool was drained and the trees felled, but Hieaway Wood remains much as it was, and for the benefit of the Pytchley I would say that Hieaway is Clint Hill Wood, near Brixworth, little over a mile from the present new Kennels which are so beautifully designed and laid out to the north of the village.

It is in Hieaway that my story opens and where Rufus was born, it is in Hieaway, it ends. Many a winters gloaming I have lain under its privet bushes listening to the wind in the dark firs and watched the little finches coming in to roost and the wheeling pigeon flocks.

Old Poors Gorse has gone, but there are parts of Blueberry bushes which remain and which still provide foxes with unerring regularity.

The lake in Maidwell Dales is dry but the brook by Lamport station which Rufus crosses on his last run, still flows and is little changed. But, alas! only the bare bones of the Rufus country of this story remain. I suppose other woods have grown up and certainly the supply of foxes—many of them descendants of Rufus—is as good as ever, despite the advance of the town and the spoilation of the countryside.

Vast new reservoirs have appeared here and there. The 'fires of Corby' which Rufus saw from afar on his nightly wanderings are larger and with a greater glare, and the 'village' of Corby is now a sprawling industrial city which eats outwards into the countryside every year.

Not only have the woods and fields changed out of all recognition. The countryside of 1938 was a more peaceful one. There were stooked fields at harvest time, and horse-drawn binders, and hay fields, lying in sweet swathes under the June sun; the hedgerows were often tall and ragged where now no hedges are visible, for hedge laying is costly and brings no return to the farmer's pocket. The oaks are being poisoned in the big woodlands because they do not promise a quick financial return, rustic carollers no longer tramp the dark and wintry lanes at Christmastide. Hideous pylons march across the open uplands where once Rufus hunted so happily under the moon.

But Fawsley park remains much as it was at the time of my story for I was there not so long ago, and maybe, if the inquisitive rambler seeks long enough, he can still discover the tombstone of the Pytchley hounds which were drowned in the lake below the ruined house. But it will take some finding in the neglected shrubberies.

Finally, there is one thing which may interest readers. In the first version of *Wild Lone* Rufus was killed by hounds, at the end of the great run, in Hieaway Wood. But my publishers urged that he should be spared. So Rufus gains the sanctuary of his kennel under the big fir.

But I leave it to the reader to decide for himself whether it was indeed Rufus, the one-eared fox, which emerged long after hounds had left, or whether it was his shadowy spirit which 'steals down into the valley fields' under the watching stars.

"BB" March 1969

CONTENTS

Foreword
		page
chapter 1.	The Spring of Life	1
2.	The Lessons of Life	21
3.	The Great Fear	41
4.	Winter Woods	59
5.	The New Year	77
6.	Summer Huntings	97
7.	The Tragedy of the Ice	109
8.	Alarms and Excursions	121
9.	Under the Stars	137
10.	In the Byre	147
11.	Halcyon Days	167
12.	Gipsy Lane	181
13.	Mystery of Penny Plain	193
14.	Snow in the Forest	205
15.	The Happy Life	219
16.	The Trap	229
17.	The Last Summer	239
18.	The Last Chapter	249

ILLUSTRATIONS

FULL PAGE PLATES

1. More often he had the scented tree aisles to himself — *frontispiece*
2. Rufus drinking in the woods — page 29
3. To a black pool in the woods some wild duck came in the evening — 45
4. Winter set in early that year — 63
5. Watchful sentinels had been posted — 83
6. A nightingale came to the whitethorn — 89
7. Living the life he loved so well — 115
8. Little was seen of Rufus — 125
9. Jogging to the meet at Houghton — 157
10. They were covered with coarse yellow down — 179
11. On his way to Hieaway — 187
12. The earth was white — 211
13. He went down slowly — 263

HEADPIECES

chapter
1. Vixen and Cubs — page 3
2. The Reaper — 23
3. Autumn Fires — 43
4. Rufus in Hieaway — 61
5. Wood Anemones — 79
6. Coldhangar Bluebells — 99
7. Rufus stalking Mallard — 111
8. Kingfisher waiting for Minnows — 123
9. Bellamy Bill, the Woodhall Poacher — 139
10. "Gone Away" — 149
11. Spring Tide — 169
12. Ploughing near Blueberry — 183
13. Wildwood Pool — 195
14. Off to draw — 207
15. A Byfield Rook — 221
16. Rufus hunted — 231
17. Summer Heats — 241
18. Hounds crossing Lamport Park — 251

TAILPIECES

Dead Vixen	20
Fir-cone	40
Fox Cub in dead Bracken	57
Wood Mouse	75
The Bellringer	95
Water Daisy	107
Wood-pigeon on Ivy	120
Young Blackbird	135
Fir Branch	146
Catkins	166
Snowdrops	178
Wild Violet	191
Chestnut Sprig	203
Fox Cub	217
Oak Sprig with Acorns	227
The Trap	237
Young Swallows	247
Endpiece	268

Chapter One
THE SPRING OF LIFE

*This was his life.
A world of scent, of rotting leaves,
And the autumn fungi round the trees;
Byfield rookery's fouled spring floor,
And thistly fields where land is poor.*

IT WAS a March evening in Hieaway Wood, and the light seemed to linger interminably. The thin, rather ragged oaks were unmoved by the slightest suggestion of breeze and, where the sandy rising ground was bare of privet bushes, the tall Scotch firs stood dark and silent, almost watchful, on top of the big mound.

Fir-cones were scattered around on the sandy soil, also little rotten fir twigs, and close to the exposed roots of one of the trees some draggled white wing-feathers of a chicken. It was the time of day when the wood-pigeons come in to roost, and now they were wheeling in a rushing grey cloud round and round the wood. Suddenly, and at the same moment, they swept back their wings, and all landed in a clappering, bustling cloud in the tops of the oak trees farther down the wood. It was quite a minute before every bird had settled down. Some had perched on thin, whippy branches and, being heavy birds, strove for a moment or two to retain their balance, bending this way and that and flapping their wings. When all were at rest, a strange hush fell, and in the exquisite silence a far song-thrush was singing. The pigeons, after having a good look round, settled down to digest their evening meal before retiring to bed. They had been feeding on a neighbouring field of greens, and their crops were stuffed with tender leaves. Under the oaks their droppings had whitened the dead leaves, for the trees had been the roosting-place of the pigeons since

November and they had not been disturbed. Some of these dead oak leaves were mere skeletons, but underneath, if you had stirred them apart, you would have found shiny, damp leaves well preserved, the colour of rich mahogany and with a wonderful aromatic scent.

A little owl began to call, somewhere outside the wood, a curious monotonous "Hooo, hooo," repeated at half-minute intervals, and a Greater Spotted Woodpecker tapped a dead oak branch that was outlined against the soft sky. "Whack, whack, whack"; the sound carried a long way. In the thick box bushes little passerine birds were rustling and hopping, preparing for the night. This was always a lengthy business, this finding of a comfortable perch, and it always took them about half an hour to settle down. A diminutive brown-barred wren was questing the sooty box roots; his bright eye seemed to miss nothing. And now he became very interested in something he saw on the sandy bank below. Inquisitive, he whirred on bee-like wings to a fallen branch that sprawled at the foot of one of the firs, and there he bobbed up and down, peering and peering. Then, "churring" in a loud, proclaiming voice, he shot like a big insect over the mound and vanished into the hollies at the foot of the slope.

At the sudden loud sound, the fox cub, which had just ventured to the lip of the earth, whisked back into the dark shadows of the hole. But very soon there was a movement in the gloom of the earth and he appeared again. Finding all quiet, he emerged on to the lip of the bank, raising his head and lowering it again, and looking on all sides with big, wide, babyish eyes. His big ears stood out like sails. Getting bolder, he scratched the back of his head with his hind leg, and the vigorous action made him feel very grown up. Shaking his diminutive woolly body, he skipped out on to the root of the adjacent fir and sniffed the chicken wing. Then he took hold of the splintered piece of bone and worried it with savage little growls.

Another little, wide-open face appeared in the mouth of the

earth, and then another, and soon four cubs were rolling and tussling with the chicken wing.

Of all the babies of the wild, the fox cub at the age of four weeks is perhaps the most attractive. His eyes have that same wondering look that one sees in very small babies of the human species, and his body is far more attractive.

While this play was going on beside the earth—little roly-poly bodies tussling and worrying—a shadow stole up the bank behind. One moment the space between the box roots and the knotted roots of the pine revealed a background of underbrush, holly and privet, and now a vixen was framed in the opening, looking down on the playing cubs. She sat for two minutes watching her children through eyes that seemed mere slits, and there was something almost cat-like in her expression, and her position was cat-like too—front paws together and her brush curled round her behind. She was lean and rather mangy, because the hunting was not good. Most of the rabbits in the vicinity had been wiped out by disease, due to over-breeding, and she was forced to hunt far afield to satisfy the wants of her growing family, and the bearing and suckling of her cubs had lowered her condition.

After looking at the playing cubs, she slid over the bank and joined them. At her approach the cubs ceased to tumble about and rushed at her, all trying to get to her teats at once. She snapped at them and pushed Rufus, who was more persistent than the others, on one side with her paw. It was only a gentle tap, but he rolled over twice, with little whimpers.

She went across to the chicken wing and sniffed it (it was the last meal she had brought her cubs the day before, and she had been so hungry that she had eaten the major part herself). The cubs came scrambling after her, still trying to burry between her legs, but she kept them gently away from her, avoiding them with easy, graceful twitches. Her husband, an old fellow in his fifth year, was a lazy father and rarely helped her with the cubs. Most of his time, when he was not sleeping off the effects of his last meal in the reeds of Lamport ponds, he was engaged in pursuing other ladies in Shortwood cover. This was one of the disadvantages of an early family (they had been born in the middle of February), but of late he had begun to bring young rabbits, though game was scarce.

The vixen lay down at the mouth of the earth, and the cubs came scrambling over her, worrying and teasing, for they were very hungry, and she had brought them no food. She stood their torment for a minute or so, then, giving herself a shake, she went down into the shadow of the earth and the cubs followed. Within, the earth was fouled by bones and droppings and smelt very badly. When she had entered, a large moth came out, flying with rather a drunken flight, for the evening was chill.

In a very short while she emerged again, with cubs still following, and slid swiftly down the sandy slope into the shadows of the box bushes, leaving her four hungry infants sitting round the mouth of the earth, gazing about with the same wondering eyes.

She skirted the box bushes and crossed the ride, entering the blackthorn thickets on the far side, scaring a blackbird that was turning over some leaves in the ditch, and sending that worthy screaming into the cover. She slipped along the hedge that led towards the railway. When she reached the thickset bounding hedge she followed this up for some way until she came to a low mound. Here she stopped and crouched low on her belly. Over the mound was a little pond fringed with rushes and overgrown with water daisies and duckweed. The vixen had noticed tracks through the green weed and the rushes smelt strongly of moor-hen. Now, when she peeped over the mound, she saw two, swimming among the weeds—the male, a fine fellow with a sealing-wax red bill pecking about with sharp jerks in mid-water, and the hen busy with the beginnings of a nest that she was constructing with great labour on a sunken tree that lay in the water. Neither bird noticed the sinister face peering over the mound, and in a second that face had vanished. Some instinct caused the female to look up; perhaps she had caught some scent, for wildfowl possess a keen sense of smell, and for a while she remained, half hunched over the mound of dead reeds beneath her belly, searching with her ruby eye the surrounding reeds and herbage. The cock bird swam over to her and climbed proudly on to the structure beside her, where he shook out his feathers and began to preen.

All this while the vixen was stealing on them from behind the bank, and now she took another stealthy peep over the top. The two birds were just below her, within springing distance, and she lay perfectly flat on the bank, the tip of her draggled brush twitching, now this way, now that. She could smell the birds, and a little dribble of saliva glistened at the corner of her mouth. Her ears were cocked forward and her whole being was tense and strung.

The cock moor-hen lifted one green red-gartered leg over a wing-covert and scratched his bill. With that sudden movement the vixen sprang. There was a wild exclamation and a shriek as the hen, turning her head at that instant, saw the body in the air, but she was too late to save her mate. One bite, and the head, with its gorgeous plated bill, dropped limply. Only a ripple showed where the hen had dived. She came up under the weeds in the middle of the pond, raising a little tent of green.

Up the rushy bank she saw the vixen slip like a shadow, the black soft body of the bird limp and warm between the ivory teeth.

Dusk had fallen when the vixen entered the wood once more. High in the firs the pigeons had dropped into roost, one by one. On the post of the hand gate sat a large grave owl, and as the vixen came up the ditch the owl swept from its perch and passed low over her head, causing her to draw back with a snarl. Many an evening the old owl had watched the cubs at the mouth of the earth, and little escaped his notice in Hieaway Wood. The vixen went straight up the bank, under the hollies and privet bushes, directly to the earth. The cubs were awaiting her round the mouth of shadow, and Rufus, always the boldest of the family though he was not the largest, came tumbling half-way down the slope to meet her. She lay for a moment with the moor-hen between her front paws, its body still warm and the eye closed pathetically by a white membrane.

Then the cubs fell upon it, growling miniature growls and tearing the flesh. Black feathers flew and floated down the sand, and the vixen withdrew to the top of the bank and lay down wearily, watching her children enjoy their meal.

After the first few days she had ceased to kennel with them in the earth and had taken to sleeping in the thick privet close by, even before her babies had opened their eyes, which was now a little over two weeks ago. This is the custom of the vixen, for the cubs give her no peace as long as she is with them, and the first rule of family life is secrecy. It was because of this too that nature ordained that the cubs' eyes should not open until much later than other animals'. Had their eyes been opened they would have wandered from the earth and fallen prey to roving vermin, including the lurcher dog from Jackman's farm on the hill behind the wood.

Suddenly she sat up, looking intently down the slope. A dark shadow was coming up over the dead leaves beneath the holly, but there was not a rustle or the snap of a twig.

It was the dog-fox, her lord and master. He had something in his jaws. She saw it was a baby rabbit, and went to meet him. Turning, she loped alongside sniffing it, and when the pair reached the earth she took it gently from him and began to eat, for she was very hungry and the cubs were full fed.

Rufus, though his little belly was as tight as any drum, came over to his mother and worried half-heartedly at the furry hind leg, but the vixen twitched the body aside and finished the meal herself, not bothering to separate the fur, but tearing pieces off and bolting them down. When she had finished she found that the fox had gone up the bank and left her, but she did not follow.

She went and lay down under the bushes, listening to all the night noises of the wood, for these were many—tiny rustles and clickings, the pat of a dropping from a roosting bird in the fir trees, the thump of a cone falling on to the dead leaves—and every now and then she would lift her muzzle and sniff the night air which brought to her so many ravishing scents. She was uneasy in her mind for her family, those little warm beings that depended on her solely for existence. Two days before she had had to slip away from under the box bushes where she was sleeping and leave her cubs. A man had come into the wood, a poacher from the neighbouring ironstone works. He had come up the sandy bank and set a snare in a rabbit run on the outskirts of the wood. He had stopped at the hole and had even knelt down and looked in. When she returned the place reeked with the hated scent that smelt of death and the end of all bright beautiful things—the wind, the night woods, warm blood and wild yearnings.

I will not say she was thinking as she lay there, but a sudden uneasiness possessed her, that grew in intensity with the passing moments. She rose and went to the earth. The bank was deserted; only scraps of fur and draggled black feathers attached to two green scaly legs remained. She entered the earth and went down into the warm reeking darkness. The cubs, sleeping off the effects of the meal, awoke and fell upon her. Without hesitating she took Rufus's little sister by the scruff of her neck and carried her out of the earth, in the same way as a cat carries its kitten. Never stopping or heeding the stifled protestations of the squirming cub, she went straight down the wood and out into the fields. Cattle were feeding, cropping the springing grass noisily in the stillness of the night, and only one mild-eyed cow saw her go past them. She stared after the shadowy apparition and then resumed her cropping of the grass. The vixen crossed the railway, delicately stepping over the metals, and struck out for Blueberry Gorse, a mile away at the foot of the hills.

It was a perfectly still night; the sky was dusted with a million eyes that seemed to watch her going, benignly and frostily aloof.

Over Coldhangar spinney, with its bare ash poles, hung the Plough, picked out against the velvet darkness, and to the south a dull glow in the sky betokened Northampton. She entered Coldhangar by the western hand gate, slipping in between the gate post and the hedge (a favourite doorway of hers, for foxes have their special openings into a wood or through a fence and will always use them, even when running before the hounds). Within, all was scented darkness, for the blackthorn bushes grew thickly right up to the edge of the woodland path, and overhead the arching thorns formed a tunnel that was gloomy even at the height of a winter's day.

Following up the path she came to a cross ride and down this she went. Once she stopped with alert, raised head as a rabbit hopped across the ride in front of her. Many times she stopped to rest her neck, for the cub was a heavy burden, even for her, and the distance was long.

At length she came to the rhododendron thickets, and up under these was a nice dry earth, dug in sandy soil and with an upper stratum of clay, which meant that it was always warm and dry. She carried the cub inside and laid it gently down, licking it twice and nuzzling it. Then she turned round and was gone. The little cub, finding itself alone with strange smells (a strange scent to a fox is as vivid as a strange sight is to us) began to whimper to itself. Then, becoming curious, it explored the new earth, but did not attempt to go up towards the mouth of the hole. Some strong instinct advised it to keep where its mother had placed it. Before very long she heard a movement up above, and Rufus was deposited, protesting loudly, by the side of his sister.

And so, during that gentle spring night, the mother vixen transferred her whole family to their new earth in Coldhangar, and when the pigeons awoke in Hieaway next morning and the light of another day filtered through the ragged oak branches, the earth beneath the big red pine was empty. Only a bluebottle was there, and he did not wake up until the pale sunlight struck the warm sandy patch. The little finches left the box bushes, twittering happily and going forth to the fields; the wood-pigeons streamed out in a body to the distant field of greens, and all of them neither knew nor cared that there were no more fox babies under the big pine.

Perhaps the big grey owl knew because he knew everything; considering he had lived in Hieaway for eighteen years he should know a thing or two. But he was not to see Rufus again for many mouse-moons, and perhaps he knew that too, "Hoo, Hoo, Knew!"

In their new quarters the cubs grew apace. Food was more plentiful because there were rabbits in the Gorse, and plenty of nests of rabbit babies were found by the vixen as the weeks mellowed in April. Beetles and mice were still scarce, so the young family subsisted chiefly on baby rabbit, varied now and then with a chicken from Jackman's farm. The dog-fox helped too, and the Hunt left him alone so that he was able, in some measure, to make up for earlier neglect.

The evenings lengthened more noticeably and all the woodland choirs sounded from valley to valley. It was a beautiful world, so full of fresh new life, of which the cubs were as much part as the lusty green shoots of the "lords and ladies" in the damp hedge-row bottoms. They began to wander farther from the shelter of the earth, and with the exercise and fine spring weather they altered in appearance. Their legs became longer and their little bodies, though still very roly-poly, showed promise of the perfected lovely creature that was to be. The full-grown fox is the most graceful and beautiful of all our truly wild animals, for coupled with that beauty of form there is an intelligence and cunning that has attracted the attention of even lordly MAN himself. He possesses the grace and sense of controlled power that one sees in some of the big game —the tiger and the panther.

The cubs varied both in size and coloration. Rufus had

scarce a trace of tag to his little brush and he was slightly smaller than his brother and two sisters. Also he was of a darker hue, even when he was but a day or two old; but he made up for his lack of size by his boldness and inquisitive nature. Though he was smaller than the others he was just as strong when it came to tearing his meat. It was Rufus that first caught a beetle. He had wandered off on his own, sniffing about under the rhododendrons, and had suddenly seen something stirring beneath a black twig. He turned the twig with a nervous little poke of his paw, and a shiny blue-cased beetle scrambled hurriedly over the leaves. He pounced forward with ears cocked and with his absurd little brush lifted, pinning the beetle to the ground with his paw. Then, with tiny growls, he bit at it with his pin-point teeth and took the beetle into his mouth; but the hard wing-cases were distasteful and he spat it out again. However, after sniffing at it for some time, he took it again into his mouth and swallowed it. Those long spring evenings seemed to last for ever in Coldhangar. The cubs, when tired of play, would sit and listen to the evening vespers of the throstles, peering and watching every passing bird and lifting their little muzzles to catch all the splendid scents of a woodland spring.

One evening, when the cubs were six weeks old, their mother brought them a great cockerel, all resplendent in burnished green and reds, and that same evening, when the night was an hour old, the dog-fox came up the bank with a white hen. Both these hapless birds were from Jackman's farm over the valley, and Mr. Jackman was a very angry man next morning. Moreover, he was fond of his fowls, and even though his rather heavy bills were paid up without murmur by the Hunt Secretary, he decided that this must stop.

Next night the cubs heard their mother coming up the bank with a good deal more noise than was her wont, and she came, not light-footed, full of the heat and fire of life, but a creature mortally stricken. Through her senses she relied on her awareness of the world, the greenness of this paradise of scent and sound; now within her all was fire and agony and a mistiness. Her last instincts took her to her dependent babies under the big rhododendrons which were already knotting up to glorious fulfilment of exotic bloom. They scrambled delightedly down to greet her, snapping and snarling with anticipation, but she could not see them now because of the mists of death. She lay on the bare earth that had nurtured her, and she lay without complaint, with only the agony in her beautiful eyes. At her final urgent convulsions the cubs delightedly skipped and frisked, for they thought she was in playful mood too.

But with a final kicking thrust of her slim black legs she lay still, and the cubs ceased to play. They sat round her with cocked ears, then, finding she did not move, they began to play with themselves, though every now and then one would run to her and worry at her teats. But the beautiful machine, so complicated, and to the slow building of which so much had been devoted, was arrested for ever. Behind the tall ash poles, already knobby with sticky buds, the pale afterlight lingered, and a distant thrush sang a requiem for the bright departed spirit.

The cockerel and the white hen had long been eaten. A whole soft spring day passed and one scented night. A yellow brimstone, the first butterfly of summer, had gone floating down the ride on wings that might have adorned a cherub in Heaven, so beautifully were they fashioned; but no fox had come to the high warm bank under the rhododendron bushes. Outside the earth the cubs were slipping uneasily about. Rufus had searched ravenously for beetles and found none; but he had been badly frightened by a hedgehog, rootling for worms under the moist leaves of the big dark bushes.

He came on it in the twilight, this mysterious ball of delightfully scented thorn. First it had run with a quaint swiftness, but, when Rufus had leapt at it in puny rage, it had curled up into a provocative thicket of thorns and one had pricked his nose. He fled, yapping in infant terror, to the shelter of the earth. Ten yards away, under the wide sweeping branches, lay the dead vixen, the bluebottles already busy with their grisly task. Several times during the day he had visited her and so had the other cubs, but they could get no response and were filled with fearful terrors and a strange smell that gave them no pleasure. They did not play now with the old fire of bursting energy, these little starving babies, only their great eyes burned with a wonder that was feverish and pitiful. At the end of the second day, his brother died, in the earth. And during the night his sister died too.

Rufus was not destined by the mysterious gods to perish, for those same laws of chance or Providence, what you will, that govern the lives of men as well as every living thing that creeps and flies and grows, had given to him that little extra inquisitiveness, that atom more energy of mind and body that was to preserve the guttering and dipping flame of life.

On the third morning Rufus, unable to stand the gnawing pangs that assailed his little body, came feebly out of the earth and went across to where the remains of his mother lay. He pushed her body with his muzzle, but so feeble was he that he hardly moved the draggled fur. Under her he saw something moving; it was a burying beetle, Nature's sexton, and in a moment he had flicked it on to its back with his paw, and eagerly devoured it. Digging with both feet he unearthed four more, and these were also rapidly disposed of.

For a short while that tiny grain of fuel kept the flame still flickering, but he was getting very weak and soon could not go more than a few feet from the earth. The other cub died during that night and Rufus was the last spark that smouldered.

Four miles away, at the foot of the green field that lay below Jackman's farm, Jackman was burying something with a spade. It was the father of Rufus, and the farmer had only just found the body of the dog-fox, lying where he had died, with a mass of white chicken feathers scattered among the green shoots of sorrel in the damp ditch. The job finished, Jackman shouldered his spade and walked across the marshy field to the lane that led across the water meadows and the river to the wooded heights of Cottesbrook.

It was a lovely sunny afternoon, and over the gold-lichened roofs of the farm outhouses the first swallow was sweeping on sable wings, chattering happily of all the lovely summer days that were hotfoot on the way. Jackman climbed the gate and dropped into the lane and was immediately aware of Miss Pamela, clad in tweeds, and accompanied by two white Highland terriers, who immediately evinced considerable interest in Mr. Jackman's spade. A guilty flush slowly swelled under his brown tan.

"Oh, good afternoon, Mr. Jackman. I've just been up to the farm to see you about the wire; I see you still have some by the lower meadow. Can't you possibly take it down? It's the last meet next week, and you may remember I saw you about it in the autumn."

"Well, Miss Pamela, it's a funny thing you should say that. I've just been there myself, sinking a gate post, and I sees the wire on my way up. I said to myself, Miss Pamela hadn't better see that or she'll be worritin' at me to get it down. I'll see to it to-morrow; I've just been waiting for the posts to come as Mr. Hendrick ordered, and I'll get the whole lot down."

"Oh, thank you ever so much, Mr. Jackman. It's so good of you. Isn't it a perfectly heavenly afternoon? I'm just going round by Coldhangar. Such a lovely day for a walk!"

Rufus was outside the earth. The pale sunlight caressed him, but he was cold, so cold. His big yellow eyes seemed not so large as usual, and within his little being the fires were flickering and dipping. One by one, wood-pigeons dropped in, perching on the ash-tree tips and cooing one to the other, happy sleepy sounds. Infant lambs proclaimed to the world ill-treatment by their woolly dams and the faint querulous sounds reached the warm bank. But Rufus did not hear them. It seemed as if he was to be an example of the waste of Nature one sees every year—the young, strong shoot that promised so well but was eaten off by a passing animal; the dead blue fledgling, lying beneath the green, mossy nest of the woodland thrush. A grey squirrel, bounding with arched tail in the grass of the ride, suddenly vanished up a nearby tree trunk, like some conjurer's trick. The pigeons, that had up till that moment been cooing and discussing love matters, all took clappering wing. A jay screamed. Something was disturbing the woodland folk.

Pamela came up the bank slowly, the white Highlands scuffling under the rhododendron bushes. Rufus did not hear the approach until they were quite close. His senses were dulled. The white Highland, Peter, saw him first and let out a wild bark. The strange fox smell excited him, and he did not at first run in and bite, and before he could do so Pamela had him by his scarlet collar. Then he leaped and strained, his excited yaps half-strangled in his throat. The other dog was too engrossed with the finding of the dead vixen to join them, and Pamela, therefore, had time to pick up Rufus and hold him against her warm body. He tried to squirm feebly and bit, but he was so weak that he soon gave up and lay still. Only in his eye and in the faint tremors of the wasted little body did she know he was frightened. Had Pamela arrived a few hours later he would have just lain in her arms with glazing eyes. The girl went down on her knees by the earth and saw the body of one of the cubs just inside. Then Peter led her over to the vixen and she knew the truth.

Within three days Rufus took a piece of rabbit from Pamela's hand, and by the end of the week he would run to meet her when she entered the stable door. But strangers alarmed him and sent him cowering into the corner among the hay. He had many human visitors, however, and soon became less nervous, though the smell of humans always filled him with a certain disgust and dislike. Had he been reared from a very tiny baby this would not have been so. At nights he was very miserable. He would prowl round and round the stable, sniffing and scratching, and he used to lie with his muzzle under the crack of the door, smelling the sweet scents of the night. In the next loose box was a hunter, and the banging and kickings sent him scurrying into the hay as the horse struck the walls with his hoof. For hours at a time he would lie in the darkness on the cold stone listening to the owls. Then he would scratch and gnaw at the base of the wooden wall that stood between him and the world outside. With the plentiful supply of food, pieces of chicken with the feathers still adhering, likewise parts of unskinned rabbits, he continued to grow in stature.

Sometimes in the quiet darkness of night he could hear mice gnawing the woodwork, and he would stalk them with stealthy tread, ears pricked and eyes staring. In one corner of the stable, where the shadow of a manger concealed it from view, there was a hole, and the mice used to venture out of this, sometimes even during the day, when Rufus was lying curled up asleep in the hay. After a while he became skilful at catching them, lying by the hole and nipping them as they streaked across the corrugated tiled floor. But it was by the door he would be, most of the night, drinking in the sweet cold rush of air as it poured in under the crack.

Once, when Pamela came to feed him in the evening, something came up to the door after she had closed it behind her, and sniffed and blew and whimpered at the crack. This something had a fearful smell which made the hair stand up along his back, and he growled savage little growls and backed away into the hay. On the other side of the door, Ruby, the foxhound pup, was down on her belly, tail swinging frantically, and giving long, snuffling breaths as the scent of the fox cub filled her nostrils with vague urgent desires. But even Pamela, who loved wild creatures and who understood them, was unable to tame the savage, independent spirit of Rufus. Though he would take food from her hand, and even, after some days of captivity, would play with her shoe-laces and nip the slim, silk-clad ankles, he would never allow himself to be picked up, but would rush away into the corner.

It soon became apparent to Pamela that Rufus was now able to look after himself, that to hold him prisoner any longer would be both useless and cruel. During his period of captivity he had been filled with miseries, a longing for the night woods and the clean air, uncontaminated by the ugly scent of humankind. And those days were days of utter boredom. Always the same smells, horses, dogs, human beings. The latter varied in an extraordinary degree; for instance, the groom who sometimes came into the stable and teased him, had a much stronger scent than Pamela. It was a harder, more ugly smell, and he associated it with physical pain. The smell of Pamela was the same human smell, but a cleaner, happier smell, and mingled with the scent of unnatural flowers. Also with this Pamela-smell was associated food, rabbit legs and nice tough chicken legs which meant great fun, worrying and tearing and forgetting his misery.

But for the greater part of the day he was alone, with only the buzzing flies that settled on the whitewashed ceiling, or which came fussing round the scraps of meat that were left over from the last meal. He would stalk these flies with great care, but they were harder to catch than mice or beetles.

In one corner of the stable was a ladder that led up to a hay-loft. Sometimes the groom would come in and, after teasing Rufus, climb the ladder. He would hear him walking about up above, and little bits of dust and plaster came wavering down. In this loft, too, there lived Pipeete, the bat, who used to emerge in the middle evening and fly round the ceiling once or twice before flickering out through the skylight over the door. Beyond these incidents there was nothing but a blank misery and dullness.

So, one still gloaming, when the light in the skylight dimmed to a pale saffron, and the blackbirds were "zinking" in the shrubberies outside, Rufus heard mingled steps coming over the stable yard. He heard and smelt Pamela, and another gruff human smell was with her. The door opened very gently and he heard whispering voices. Pamela came over to him as he sat upright by the scaly leg of a chicken. By the door stood a black and white shadow, from which came the strong man smell, and he would not move. Pamela bent over him, talking in a soft voice and stroking him gently down the centre of his head; but he backed away into the corner and sat alert and watchful until Pamela walked over and joined the man by the door. After five minutes, as neither figure moved, Rufus began to scent the night air. Through the door which now stood so wide open he could see a stretch of cobbled yard and the corner of a laurel shrubbery. One other black and white figure, Pamela's father, stood watching by the back door of the house. Somewhere in another stable, Ruby was proclaiming to the world the injustice of mankind—she could smell her people standing in the yard and she had been locked away. A horse whinnied from a nearby stall, and this seemed suddenly loud in the silence.

Up above this scene, Pipeete, the bat, circled and wavered, now swooping low past the eaves of the stables, now flittering round the tall lime trees on the drive. Rufus still sat in his corner, distrustful and afraid. Of a sudden something turned the balance within him, and first trotting forward delicately towards the open door, he stopped again, watching the silent figures standing in the yard. The slim, rather boyish figure of Pamela shining white in the dusk, the black and white figures of the motionless men. In the hand of one of the men Rufus saw a glowing red eye and this is what held him. It shone like the eye of some sinister creature that was waiting to spring on him if he dare venture out. With his three weeks' captivity he had come to regard his corner under the manger as his den. Then, like a brown shadow slipping along the wall, Rufus was gone.

One moment he had been in view of the waiting watchful figures, a little slip of tense life poised like a runner awaiting the shot, next moment and the threshold of the stable was empty.

Four hours later Pamela threw wide the window and leant out, gazing into the garden below. The spring night was pregnant with sweet scents, and the gilly-flowers along the terrace perfumed the still air. In the moonlight the bare limes stood, their branches speckly with green unfurling leaves, and Pipeete, the bat, was still flickering in the gentle duskiness.

Beyond the terrace the lawns fell away, the new-mown surface adding its quota of scent to the night, and beyond the lawns the steep valley, smoking in white mists.

She thought of the empty stable, with the remains of the last meal, the faint foxy smell that was now gradually to fade. A white ghost passed along the edge of the lower lawn, hovered like a cloud for a moment, then passed on; it was the barn owl who lived in the elm tree at the bottom of the drive.

"Where is he now . . . where is he now!" So mused the girl with the quiet eyes.

Chapter Two
THE LESSONS OF LIFE

Scent of the walnut leaves in May,
And the lime trees' breath at the close of day.
Smell of the river, willow bound,
Rabbit run, and a questing hound.

NOW—the first week in June—and the ashes in Coldhangar making up their minds to come into full leaf. Two weeks had passed since that night when Rufus gained his freedom, and he was alive and flourishing. With no one to teach him he had found the way to catch beetles under the flat, dry cakes of cow dung in the fields, and for a week he had lived almost entirely on them. In the marshy ground by the Nene, he had found frogs, and though at first the jumping odd-smelling creatures had scared him, he had sampled one and found them, if not of excellent flavour, at least passable, and he was tired of beetles and worms.

In the dew-wet grass by Coldhangar spinney, Rufus was slipping along, his back pads carefully placed in the prints of his fore-feet. He was very hungry, the diet of frogs and beetles did not sustain him long; his belly ached for warm blood and flesh. Along the side of the gorse the rabbits were out in hundreds and he could see their white scuts bobbing about him on all sides in the starlight. Again and again he tried to stalk them, but they always ran away before he got within striking distance.

Following the fence, and stopping every now and then to sniff the night air, Rufus came to the gate at the top of the gorse cover, and here there was a sharp angle of the railings before they sloped downhill. He approached this with caution because his nose told him a rabbit was just over the rise. Crouching low on his belly he crept up to the corner where a large clump of nettles showed blackly as they sprouted out from beneath the railings. Peeping over the top he saw the tips of a rabbit's ears, little more than a foot away. It was busy feeding and had its back to Rufus. With every nerve and sinew strung for the leap, Rufus lowered his body, and then, like a released spring he landed on the rabbit's back, biting at its neck. But Rufus was still a cub scarcely half grown, and the rabbit was a buck, and a tough old buck at that. With a scream it leapt a foot into the air, and Rufus was sent tumbling against the fence. In a flash, however, he was on his feet and after the rabbit as it ran into the gorse. The bite had not been sufficient to paralyse, but it had drawn blood, and as the rabbit ran, mazed and half conscious, the blood trickled down in beads on to the bare, hard earth. A rabbit, even if hard pressed, will usually make for its own burry, though there may be others close at hand, and this rabbit lived some way down the gorse thicket, close to the wire fence.

With Rufus hard on his heels he went under the wire again, into the open field where the going was better. Scattered about were ant-hills (dearly loved by the green woodpeckers in Cold hangar in the sunny hours) and between these mounds the rabbit raced. He was weak from loss of blood, and close by the foot of one of the ant-hills Rufus was on to him again like a little demon. But the rabbit, with a twist of its body, threw the cub aside again, and lashed out with its strong back legs. The blow caught Rufus square in the muzzle, and sent him whimpering under the wire. With lowered tail he crouched for a moment, then sprang out again to the ant-hill. But the rabbit was not there, only some drops of blood and tufts of grey fur.

Baffled and angry, Rufus went on down the slope, threading his way between the ant-hills and stopping every now and then to peer about him. Here, at this spot, the grass grew in dead tufts intermingled with new shoots. His ears suddenly caught a faint rustle in the grass, a sound which would be beyond the range of any human ear, but clear enough to Rufus. He froze, ears pricked forward and back in a curve, with brush rather straight out behind. His whole attitude was of intense concentration. There was something rustling in the grass which was bigger than a beetle. A fox can see at night as well as a human being can see during the day, and even though it was not moonlight the minute shakings of the grass were noted by Rufus, who had raised himself on his hind legs to get a better view.

He sprang, catlike, and landed with both front paws together. Something gave a feeble cheep, and keeping his paws still—purely by instinct—he felt the mouse's body, warm and soft under his pads. It was dead, and he ate it greedily, lying down on his stomach in the dew-wet grass. He felt the warm blood on his tongue as the frail little body burst, and he gave a savage throttled growl. After finishing his meal he walked quietly down by the side of the fence, his young body tingling with this new-found joy, the hunting joy that of all the experiences of his life was to be the most vivid. To be hungry with the hunting hunger, and to appease that hunger with warm blood—there was never to be anything so vivid as that.

Up in Coldhangar the vixen used to bring them mice alive, and even fledgling birds, for her cubs to kill. But this was a different thing.

After indulging in the luxury of a scratch and a lick round his whiskers, he went on down towards the wooded knolls of Blueberry. The summer night was heavy with scent. In the semidarkness the white snow of the may shone out from every hedge, and the crab-apple trees were in flower too. He entered Blueberry by the same way his mother used, by the hand gate on the south side. He could not have known that this was the vixen's road, but some instinct told him to use that gateway, and he slipped between the post and the bank as though he were an old fox. Underfoot the moss was soft and deep, that lovely woodland moss which is so sought after by the woodland thrushes. He trotted along the path, ears pricked and alert in every sense, and every now and then he stopped to listen and sniff the air.

The night was full of sound. In the upper woods owls were hooting, calling one to the other with mournful quavering cries, and a young tawny was perched on a dead tree close to the ride, calling for food. It made the most extraordinary noise, a kind of hissing screech that was repeated with monotonous regularity. Rufus was mystified at this sound and rather frightened. For some minutes he stood with one paw raised. After a while he crept forward under the thick thorns until he was directly under the stump. He could not see the bird because it was a long way above him, hidden by a bulge in the trunk; but as he watched, a big, brown shadow swept across the open space of stars and joined the youngster on the dead branch. Then the hissing sound was trebled, and a little bit of rotten wood came ticking down the tree, and landed on the soft moss at the feet of Rufus. He jumped back, then went gingerly forward again and sniffed it. The mother owl swept away on mothy wings, and the youngster followed. Rufus heard the wheezing hiss die away through the night woods. He left the path and slipped along beneath the impenetrable walls of thorn. Tracks of the woodland folk were everywhere and he could smell rabbit in many of the runs.

He had got half-way down the slope of the wood when he suddenly heard a most terrible noise. It was, at first, far away, in the upper edge of Blueberry where the ash poles begin. It was a terrible wailing scream, like a creature in fearful torment. It began with a whine and climbed the scale, then died away in grunting gurgles. In the silent midnight woods it would have been an appalling sound to a human being, but Rufus was simply interested. In fact, to him it seemed rather a nice noise, and awoke in him a warm, hungry feeling. He stopped under the thorn tangles, listening. Up above, in the angle of a spiky thorn, was a large, green nest. A mother song-thrush was brooding her five half-naked babies, and her eye grew round and suspicious in the dim light. Her sharp ears had caught the sound of the wailing cry and she turned her head from side to side, listening intently. Perhaps she was aware, too, of the sinister little shadow beneath, listening with cocked ears to the same cry.

As the minutes passed the horrible sound came nearer. Whatever it was, animal or disembodied spirit, it was coming up the steep bank where the foxgloves grew, and where the trees gave way to a bracken-covered clearing. Rufus heard a stick crack in the distance, and a curious grunting sound. Still bold, still interested, he trotted to meet this spirit of the night. He came to the edge of the thorn brake, and from there he could see down the woodland path, looking now like a tunnel in the dim light. Out of the tall spires of willow herb and sturdy foxglove, a thick-set bear-like creature emerged, and its head was blazed black and white. It came up the path with a shuffling, clumsy gait, head low, seeming to move on jerky castors. Rufus shrank back under the thicket, ears cocked and eyes starting. Old Brock, the boar badger, went by without noticing anybody. From time to time he would stop and sniff the moss and herbage by the side of the path, but in a few moments he went out of sight behind the bend in the path.

The short summer night was nearly over. To the east a faint paleness appeared, and very soon the first notes of the song-thrushes, the heralds of the dawn, came from the thickets on top of the high mound. A wren sang loudly, its song for an instant drowning all other sounds. The chill of the dawn's breath came also, and the mother song-thrush on her nest in the blackthorn raised herself and turned round on her youngsters. One of them pushed its gaping head between the side of the nest and the spotted flank, and wagged a moment. Then it sank down into the warmth and darkness of the brooded nest.

Blackbirds warbled very quietly, and the wood-pigeons started to coo in the ash poles. The world was waking up, and Rufus, still hungry, turned up the bank and curled up under the thick rhododendrons. "Cuckoo, Cuckoo." The clear notes seemed to match the summer dawn which was creeping so freshly over the green world. Summer dawn in the woods, where no man came! The wild woodland folk waking up! What a beautiful, beautiful world! But under the dark spreading leaves the cub was asleep. His nose was curled round to his brush, like a dog, and his sides moved with the regularity of his breathing.

When the sun came up, the bushes and thickets became alive with busy birds: birds singing, birds building, birds flying off to feed their families, birds love-making, birds preening. The insects awoke too. A big velvet bee came humming along up the bank, the tiny particles of dead leaves and grass moving under the vibrating air of his wings, and the deep humming made the cub twitch in his sleep. The cuckoo came and perched in a spreading may tree close by the rhododendrons, and his clean shouting made the woodland ring. But Rufus slept on. A spider came over the leaves, a big spider, with legs so thin and long they acted as shock absorbers to the round body in the centre, much as a carriage body is slung on springs. It came over the leaves and crawled over the cub's nose; he only shook his head and one hind leg twitched. A jay screamed like a piece of tearing calico, twice, in the rhododendron bushes. Perhaps he smelt the cub. He did not see him, for a moment later he flew away on dipping rounded wings, his china-blue eye scanning the thickets of thorn for nests. Rufus slept on.

Throughout the whole of that hot summer day Rufus slept under the rhododendron bushes. True, he changed his resting-place several times and left his card at the base of a clump of sprouting bracken, but the busy day passed uneventfully. Out in the hot fields, among the ant-hills, the green woodpeckers hunted for ants, flying to and fro between the woods and meadows with dipping

Rufus drinking in the woods

flight. A farmer came with his dog, herding sheep, and the barking and baa-ing roused Rufus from his slumbers. But the sounds died away, and only bird and insect songs filled the drowsy air.

In the green nest, built in the fork of the blackthorn, the gaping young thrushes jostled each other in their greed as the parent birds went to and fro with food. One, lifting its stern over the edge to evacuate, hoisted itself too far and fell with a thump on the moss. It lay there, feebly moving for three hours, and all the time the thrushes went back and forth overhead and took no heed.

When the rich mellow notes of the nightingale began to sound down the woodland aisles, Rufus awoke, very hungry. A faint breeze brought him the scent of bird, and he went down the bank to investigate. He soon found the young thrush and it was better than the mouse. After eating it, he smelt all round the moss, then looked upwards at the bright green mass of the nest. Although he knew there were other tasty morsels there, he could not climb, so he stood up, with his two front paws on the base of the prickly tree, but he could only peer and strain. The two parent thrushes soon spied him, and made the evening loud with their cries. A cock blackbird heard the commotion and came over to see what it was all about, and soon there was an hysterical ring of birds shouting at him, flying from bush to bush, and peeping down at him. This brought a jay over, and two magpies, and there was such a hideous din that Rufus was really terrified. He ran swiftly up the bank again, and hid in the rhododendrons until the hubbub died down.

That night he caught three mice and found another baby bird, a magpie, that had fallen out of the nest in the top of one of the ash poles. It was rather "high," and the bluebottles had been busy in the carcase, but it tasted better than the mice, and he finished up everything save the claws and beak. Truly, Rufus was finding his feet, and life was good, very good.

As summer advanced into July, game was more and more plentiful, and most of Rufus's fare consisted of young creatures that could not fly or run because of undeveloped wings and legs. The mortality among the babies of the woodland folk is appalling, for besides foxes, stoats, jays, and owls taking their toll, magpies are perhaps the worst offenders.

As the days advanced Rufus grew with the good fare. By now he was standing well off the ground, and his brush was quite long and bushy, though still lacking the usual white tip that is found on the average fox's brush. His coat had lost the woolly lamb-like quality of babyhood, and his movements were graceful and lithe.

One evening, in the hedgerow below Coldhangar, where the alders were already flowering in broad, yellow plates that tainted the air with sweet-rank scent, he smelt a sudden puff of warm bird. It was different from the usual bird smell because it was more gamey, like a bird that had lain for a while and ripened. He stopped, but the smell vanished, and he could only smell the alder which seemed to drown everything. Down in the ditch, amongst the tangle of nettles and briars, the mother partridge had raised herself for a moment on her newly hatching babies, a very late brood (her first effort in May had been destroyed by a hunting stoat). That movement was to be fatal. On the bank above, the fox cub was raising himself, and peering down, his head bent sharply at an angle to his neck and his ears cocked like question marks. His sharp eyes detected some brown streaked feathers, only half a square inch, between a gap in the nettle stalks, but it was enough. He sprang, and for a moment there was a wild, silent battle in the bottom of the ditch. Rufus, half-blinded by feathers, held on grimly to a hind leg. It broke and he shifted his grip with a lightning snap, and the bundle of brown, warm feathers sagged limply. After licking the body, he turned to the nest. There were nine olive eggs; two had just chipped, and in one corner of the nest was a newly hatched chick, its feathers not yet dry.

When Rufus had finished the eggs and the babies, he was so tight that he could not hold any more. So he picked up the partridge and carried it into Coldhangar, up under the rhododendron bushes. Here he buried it, in a very haphazard fashion, because he left one broken leg sticking out of the mould and nearly the whole of one wing. Then he went higher up the wood and had a nap.

When he awoke the moon was coming up over the ash poles and dark bushes, flooding every glade and ride with silver light. Millions of moths were abroad, and over the grasses by the side of the wood white moths were weaving a fairy dance, their mating dance. And nightjars hawked on curved wings, as silent as the moths and owls. He went down to the place where he had buried the partridge, but someone was there already.

Old Brocky, the boar badger, snuffling along on his nightly hunt for garbage, had smelt the buried bird under the bushes, and now his aldermanic figure was busy in the shadows with the remains. Rufus heard the old gentleman grunting with pleasure, and eating noisily. Old Brocky did not care a rap for anybody. He went where he willed, he never troubled to walk like a hunter because he rarely stalked his game, and he lived mostly on what other people left him. But with all his apparent devil-may-care manner of life he combined a very shrewd brain, which had enabled his race to hold their own down through the ages, and now, in the most trying period of all—the age of machinery and awakened human ideas and aspirations—he still roamed the woods.

He was enjoying Rufus's partridge—*his* partridge, if you please—with the gusto of a gourmet drinking soup, and the noise, combined with the offensive smell (for old Brocky had a strong aroma) sent the hairs creeping along the back of Rufus. He crept up behind the massive grey back, and his eyes blazed with fury. He prepared to spring. All this time, old Brocky crunched and slobbered with glorious abandon. His little ears, set close to his barred head, were amusing from behind. They curved ever so slightly outwards at the tip, and gave the appearance of little horns. With a snarl Rufus sprang and in a moment the night was hideous. Things happened so quickly under the dark bushes that it was difficult to see what really did happen. The seemingly ungainly old gentleman in grey became a spring of snapping steel, and the dreadful jaws bit into the shoulder of Rufus. It was a terrible bite, no clean slashing snap, but a solid crunching bite. Rufus "ki-wied" in exquisite agony, and went rolling down the bank among the anemones. The badger, fluffed out to twice his size, stood on square legs, looking down the slope. Then, without more ado, he went on with his meal, grumbling to himself.

Rufus got to his feet and limped away. His left foreleg would not function, but hung, dangling uselessly. It throbbed and burned, and he stopped again and again to lick it. Down the woodland path he went, no longer with graceful, easy stride, but with the pitiful limping gait of a maimed animal. Across the moonlit ride the dark masses of foliage cast wide pools of inky shadow. A rabbit hopped out into a space of grey-green moonlight, and stood for a moment watching the limping fox as he came slowly down the ride. Like two interrogation marks the rabbit's ears were opened forward in a V, and he raised himself on his hind pads. Then he scurried into the underbrush.

Rufus limped on unheeding, aware only of the pricking fire in his leg and shoulder. Luckily, that terrible crunching bite had missed breaking the bones, and had only bruised them, but there was a deep gash in his shoulder from which the blood welled slowly. He lay down, exhausted and weak, under a large clump of bracken, and licked and licked unceasingly. After about an hour he heard something coming below. He lay stretched out under the ferns, with his nose along the ground, and his eyes on the moonlit path. A big sow badger, Mrs. Brocky, came trotting round the bend at a rolling waddle. Behind ran two cubs, nine weeks old. They followed their mother as a farrow of piglets follow their sow. Every now and then one would turn aside to investigate something. As the trotting sow did not stop, the cub would be left behind, and it suddenly pleaded loudly for the sow to stop. She took no heed, but went on under the fern fronds, and the cub would trot quickly after, still complaining, until it caught her up.

When the sow reached the spot to windward of Rufus she stopped, raising her pig-like snout and sniffing the air. But after a while she trotted on, making for the ash poles at the top of the cover.

When the first thrushes began to pipe up, Rufus took himself limping off to his bed under the rhododendrons. After the rest his leg was even more stiff and useless, though the pain had in some measure abated. A dull dawn came, grey and soft, and light rain dropped pattering on the leaves. It rained all that day, and the welcome moisture brought out the scents of earth and leaf. Rufus was a sick dog and did not hunt that night, and to make his sorrows more keen he had another terrifying experience which he did not understand.

Towards nightfall the rain ceased and the air grew humid and lifeless. Birds were silent in the woods, and he could hear only the drip and pat of the moisture falling from leaf and fern. Away in the distance he heard a rumbling, muttering roll, which, as the minutes passed, grew louder and louder. Soon a mysterious blaze of white light flickered through the dark trees, lighting up the shadows in an instant glare that left his eyes, for a moment, mazed. Soon the sound of the mighty explosions shook the wood, and not a sound was heard from bird or beast. All were cowering in their holes and thickets. A terrified blackbird flew past the bushes and vanished in the shadows. At each blinding flash he heard a hiss in the air, and a gunpowdery smell drifted to him. Without warning there was another blinding flash and a roar that rocked the ground. This was followed by the slow splintering, bursting crack of a stricken tree. The great oak at the top of the ride had been struck, and a branch, the mightiest of the three, had been riven from tip to base.

Rufus forgot even his stiff leg. He slipped from under the bushes and scurried out of the wood. Before he reached the open field and the ant-hills, a blinding flash lit up the whole scene, and he turned back into cover. The whole countryside had been lit up for him in that moment, revealing the wooded height of Clint Hill. Rain drops as heavy as marbles hissed down with a metallic drum, and the sound made even the shelter of the woods seem foreboding. He ran to earth under the rhododendrons, and was grateful for the darkness. He lay there trembling and shaking, his eyes and ears wide with terror. But after a while the grumbling rumbles died away. The heavy tattoo of rain ceased, and only the intermittent "drip, drip" of the moisture made the woodland seem alive.

July had come and gone. Days of heat, days of rain, the darkening of greens and silence of birds. The blossom time was over and there were no plates of rank alder any more, no crab blossom, no heavy snow of scented may. It seemed the year was tiring. Rufus was well again and more than three parts grown. With abundant food (for the woods were full of the harvest of the woodland folk just learning to fly and run) he had regained his former grace and beauty, and though he still limped ever so slightly—an unpleasant reminder to leave Brocks severely to their own wishes in future—he travelled the fields nightly for many miles around.

Rufus was no stay-at-home fox. The daring and adventurous spirit of his cubhood days when he used to explore the sandy bank of Hieaway was still with him, and the exercise and fine living was breeding in him a splendid virile strength. Though he returned every dawn to the thorn fastnesses of Coldhangar, he roamed for miles at night, becoming familiar with every spinney, farm and hedgerow within a radius of eight miles and more. He met other foxes on his nightly travels, but beyond a passing interest, he came to avoid such encounters, and hunted on his wild lone as a good fox should.

Although he explored with inquisitive nose the powerful smells of Jackman's farm, he left the chickens alone and the only thing he took from the vicinity was a poor mazed runner duck that had got shut out one night, and was spending an anxious quacking purgatory in the green duck-pond below the farm. A fox that forms bad habits in the matter of poultry raiding does not live long, but in all fairness to Rufus it must be said that he preferred to hunt in the wilds, and to catch wild game. Hunting was his greatest joy. It was no mere appeasing of hunger that delighted him; it was the sleeping country fields and spinneys, fraught with wondrous scents and abounding with tasty game that was such fun to stalk and capture.

During the hours of daylight he would sleep and dream, his legs moving sometimes in his sleep. When the owls began to hoot and the dews glistened the grass, he would slip away, hunting his passage across the meadows to the railway. It was fun, too, up the river in those late summer nights; the chuckle of the water as it swept under some half-submerged log would fill him with instant curiosity, and there were water-hens to hunt in the scented rushes, though he did not catch them. Sometimes he found the partly eaten roach and dace left by some heron or otter, mostly in a stinking condition, but very tasty. And to keep himself free of mange he ate the beetles that lived under the cow cakes in the meadow grasses. He would turn the dried cakes swiftly over with his paw, and catch the scurrying astonished creepy-crawleys clad in mail. This business of beetle hunting delighted him, and every time he turned over a cow platter it was an adventure.

Down by the river mice abounded, and when the evenings were quiet and the fields clear of man, he would hunt them for hours in the lush grass. Once, the old owl from Hieaway came upon him in the twilight and swooped at him, scaring him out of his wits, and making him draw back his lips to show his ivories. It was a carefree happy time, that July and August, and his old wound had healed completely.

The poachers from Brixworth lost many a rabbit from their snares set along the Blueberry Gorse. It was easy meat for Rufus, and there were plenty of snares. Sometimes he could not eat all the rabbit, and would bury the remains under the ash-pole tumps in Coldhangar. Sometimes he returned and dug them up, but sometimes forgot all about them, and Mr. Brocky, on his nightly rounds, put on a few more cumbrous pounds of weight.

At the end of August he took to lying out in a field of corn not far from Clint Hill. Maybe he found the woods too oppressive as summer reached maturity, maybe it was simply the novelty of change. But this habit gave him a lesson, and after that lesson he never lay out in crops again. One night, after catching a full-grown rabbit in the corn he went to sleep in his usual place, and awoke to find a menacing sound. It was a clattering rattle that sounded from all sides and made him crouch where he was, hoping it would go away. But as the day advanced it grew louder, and with it the voices of man and the smell of man. The day was sweltering and he lay, not daring to move. He watched the little insects climbing the strong columns of the wheat and the deep, red poppy heads that smelt so strange, hanging like ballet skirts above his head. During the middle of the day the clattering ceased, and he stole to the edge of the corn forest. The reaper was close by under the hedge, with the teasing flies worrying the poor horses until they were nearly driven mad. Men were there, too, sitting in the shade, laughing and talking, so he crept back into the corn stalks, praying for night and release. But in the early afternoon the clattering began again, and drew nearer and nearer in an ever decreasing radius, until he slunk this way and that in abject fear.

More voices, more noise, and the man smell stronger and stronger. Terrified rabbits went hopping past him, and little mice too, all with fear in their movements. A hedgepig was one of the beleaguered garrison, but Rufus had no heart for food or hunting. The common danger made all these wild creatures of common blood; man was ever planning their destruction.

Now the rabbits, those that were bolder than their fellows, began to break for cover. Shot after shot rang loud in his ears, mingling the smell of powder with the hated smell of man and all his works. At each shot and swish of falling corn, the hedgepig jerked into a ball, cautiously to open one eye again a moment later, and like a flustered old lady she would run off into the corn forest. Nearer came the reaper, nearer the tramp of men and horses, the smell of man sweat, horse sweat, steel, and dusty earth, red and powdery. The garrison had retreated to the last stronghold, a swathe of corn fifty yards long by five feet broad. A man with a stick came down the swathe, beating at the crouching rabbits which began to dart in and out round Rufus. But he lay with his nose straight out and heart hammering in his ears. Now . . . like a streak he was out of the corn and ran between the legs of a small urchin with bare knees. Barring his way was another man and a boy who shouted at him. But unlike the poor, stupid rabbits who lost their heads, Rufus kept his, with almost a grin on his face, and dodged the flying sticks and hobnails with graceful ease. In a moment the turmoil and the shouting was behind him—the scattered shots and discordant cries, the smell of blood and death, and the hot cornfield.

Over the railway, past Coldhangar, Bluecovert and Berrydale with its heron-haunted ponds, he went, straight as an arrow, for Scotland Wood and its dark firs that crowned the skyline. When the evening came and shadows stole down the burnt hillsides and the bobbing meadow browns went to sleep upside down on the thistle tops, Rufus was deep in the sanctuaries of the green woods, with the cool moss and bushes. Only in his mind there still lingered the agony of the afternoon, and he had learnt a lesson, one of many, with a painful vividness. Man, the enemy, the archenemy, who smelt of death and the end of green life, surely never came here to this hushed paradise.

From the boughs of a sallow bush a red-waistcoated robin suddenly let fall a tender cascade of tinkling notes, sad little notes, infinitely sorrowful and exquisitely sweet. He was singing of all the sorrows of hunted things, and the mysteries of life and death. He sang a little melody on the death of the partridge killed by Rufus in the hedge bottom, and the young magpie that had fallen from the ash pole nest in Coldhangar. He sang of the pity of helpless naked things cut off before they had known the world and life; he sang of the poisoned vixen mother of which now no trace at all remained in the world. Of the cruelty of man, too, he sang, with his tubes of death and his lust for blood. But he also sang of the nobleness of man, of the spark of humanity that still was to be found within him, of his love of nature and of wild things. He sang of the pattern of life; life for a life, because that was how life remained, feeding on itself and being born anew. He told how man is an animal, too, and must live on life, and how he controlled the lives of birds and beasts so that he was almost a god in himself, able to give life or withold it at his pleasure, even to his own kind. And he sang at last of the departing summer, and the glory of the world.

Then, giving himself a little shake, and cocking his eye on the sleeping fox to see if his song had made any impression, he flitted away through the sallows.

And Rufus, under a fallen tassel of Scotch fir, slept. Above him rose a great tree, its bark red in the evening sun; it stood like a benign God of nature looking down on this child asleep at its feet, and in the topmost branches a little wind sang softly too. . . .

Chapter Three
THE GREAT FEAR

Scent of the bloom on Old Poors Gorse,
A beaten fox, a sweaty horse,
Smells of blood, and a chicken pen,
Pheasant and mallard, water-hen.

MID-OCTOBER in Coldhangar . . . pearly mornings and mushrooms, dying hues of leaf and fern, mists coming up from the river, and longer nights for hunting! Rufus was well grown now; a lithe, clean-run fox without a trace of mange.

In the woodland rides the gold-red leaves lay deep, and with every sigh of air, more would tick and waver down as though loath to join the earth. Most beautiful of all were the pink, almost incandescent, fires of the sloe bushes, and the vivid autumn fungi that grew round the bases of the big trees.

The field maples flamed a lovely salmony orange; the exquisitely cut leaves, borne on the slender pinkish stems, seemed to mock the paintings of a Japanese artist, and the ditches were full to overflowing with millions of such little beauties, each one a picture in itself. The trees that already showed their bare bones revealed also new and hidden loveliness, yet men went about this world and were blind to it all.

There was a new exciting mystery in the woods, too; nay, in every little spinney, wherever trees gathered together. The lower veils of foliage had not yet dropped, but let through the light in a magical way, and the earth, strewn with the damp fresh-fallen leaves, took on a new smell, sweeter far than the rarest incense. This rusty wealth and range of colour blended with an enchanting rareness the hues of the fox's coat as he padded about his secret ways.

To a black pool in the centre of the woods, some wild duck came in the evenings. The pool was not deep, though it appeared so because the water was so dark and peaty-looking, due to unburdening of many autumns such as this, generations of trees shedding their leaves into its mirror. To this pool came a drake mallard, a duck and three youngsters born in April by Wildwood pool, four miles away across the fields. Every evening, when the smoke from the cottage chimneys was sending up soft blue signals, they circled the wood and came in to this dark water, and Rufus knew of this arrangement. For three nights he had lain in the dying brambles close to the water's edge at the upper end of the pond. From this ambush he had caught moor-hens, young ones, as they quested about on the black evil-smelling ooze, in which a bullock would have sunk to his middle.

On the fourth night Rufus went again and hid in his favourite ambush. For a long while nothing came but a cock bullfinch that had been piping in the maple bushes, and he came for a sip before going to bed. He was a lovely little bird, with a breast the colour of some of the hawthorn leaves and a cap as blue as a crow's wing. "Wit, Wit!" he flew up again, and only his white rump was visible as he flew away through the dark thickets.

"Hoo, hoo, hoohoo!" the owls awoke, mothy and with mothy eyes, birds of the touchwood and the night.

A wee mouse rustled, ever so quietly, making no more sound than a little brown sprite, but Rufus heard it and his eyes took on a watchful expression and both ears cocked right forward. He sat up slowly with bent head, staring through the veil of bramble leaves to where the maple bushes formed a fairy screen. But the mouse disappeared, and the fox lay down again and resumed his watch on the pond.

Whenever the shadows began to fall in the woods, the blackbirds made much bother, zinking like a pair of rusty shears.

To a black pool in the woods some wild duck came in the evening

Sometimes they had cause for alarm, especially when the owls awoke. There was nothing they liked more than teasing the owls, and they drove the poor big-headed things to distraction.

All kinds of sounds came to Rufus as he lay under the brambles, and all manner of smells, all far beyond the range of human ear and nose. He could smell a rabbit that was hopping along beyond a fallen tree-trunk on the other side of the pond; he could smell the yellow-lipped sinister fungi that grew on the underside of the fallen tree. He could recognise a moor-hen scent coming from the rushes on his right, and a dead water-rat was lying on the edge of the mud, where a little trickle of water fed the pool. He could smell other things, the scents of different plants and trees, and he sorted them all out with a twitch of his nose.

He could hear a beast scratching itself against a rubbing post outside the wood (the post was all shiny on one side and had given pleasure to countless tough hides now long perished) and the men talking over their spades in the village allotments right on the other side of the hill.

And all about there was a pattering, as of little furtive feet. This was the sound of the falling leaves, millions of them, falling all over the wood in a ceaseless flurry of yellow and amber snow. Whenever a breath of wind came over the hill the rustling would grow, and it sounded as if fairy armies were on the march. This pattering would have made a man uneasy if he had lain there long, but Rufus knew them for lifeless things.

Far singing came to him. It was a party of cyclists on the Harboro' road. They were bent over their handlebars with eyes fixed on the ground, blind to all beauty of earth and sky. They were singing a sexy American jazz song, "D'you love your baby like I love ma baby, or do you simply say, Meet me at twilight, little Miss Eyebright, then that'll be O.K." One of the cyclists was a beefy girl, and her bare lobster-tinted thighs worked like pistons. How could they guess a little red fox heard them, as he lay under the pink bramble leaves by a wood pool!

The sounds died away, and then a cow began to call, a faint horn-like sound like a man calling a moose.

Across the pool a big white owl suddenly flew, quite silently, and two blackbirds chased it. One, in its excitement, let fall a white spot into the water and the consequent rings took quite a minute to subside. Losing their quarry, the excited blackbirds came back into the holly tree close by, and one of them, dropping to the leaves for a moment, saw this new enemy. For a minute it sat there, tail slightly up and its privetberry eye fixed on the fox. Then, with a scream, "zink, zink, zink," it flew up into the tree and the other blackbird saw the fox as well. Both birds hopped low in the holly, scolding and shaking the leaves. Before very long, a mistle-thrush—a big handsome masculine bird, that feared no man nor beast, and who built in the most absurdly naked positions with such infinite scorn—came and joined the blackbirds, and his long, drawn-out rasping call was louder than the blackbirds'. As Rufus showed no sign of life they soon went away. There was no fun in teasing a thing that would not move, and perhaps the fox was dead.

"Whi, whi, whi, whi," the sound of pinions circling! Rufus became alert, his eyes glowing and tail twitching ever so slightly. The circling mallards kept on coming round and round past the holly, trying to make up their minds to land. With exasperating indecision they kept this up for two minutes; then the drake, feeling perhaps a little tired of the business, landed with a splash in mid-pond. Immediately he turned round, backing water, his neck very straight and rigid, and a semi-smile on his face, which was not really a smile at all. The other mallards immediately landed, too, and for a full minute they took stock of their surroundings. Then they began to swim slowly about, preening, questing the weeds and mud, and feeling more and more at home. But they did not come near the holly.

In the centre of the pond was a stump of a tree, very green because fresh grass was sprouting on it, and the edge of the stump was quite shiny, trodden by the feet of resting waterfowl. A few grey feathers were there too; it was an ideal preening place. The drake mallard climbed on to this with sturdy greenish-yellow legs, the colour of the rushes, and stretching his head right out and raising the feathers on his head he gave himself a good shake, just as a farmyard duck will do. Several small feathers dropped out of his person. He preened carefully, first his madder breast and then his tail, twisting round and pulling at his white outer tail-feathers.

There drifted across to Rufus the most appetising smell of wild duck and with every exertion of the preening mallard this scent seemed redoubled. It was agony for Rufus. He was ravenous, and he felt much as a hungry man would feel if a steaming turkey were put before him, and he were unable to touch it. The saliva dribbled out of the corner of his mouth, but he never moved. After a lengthy toilet, the mallard pushed off into the pond, passing some remarks in a low, watery voice to his duck. They swam about together, throwing the beads of moisture over their backs with evident abandon. But they did not come near the holly.

In the water was the reflection of a star, and soon a wondrous thing appeared. Over the tops of the thick crowding trees, rose a misty glow, and soon the moon, red and large, swam clear—the Hunter's Moon. It was reflected in the water, not as a whole, but in little shaking pieces as the ducks swam about.

Rufus was puzzled at this light and was at first a little nervous, but he soon thought of nothing but "duck" again, and how to capture one. The young mallards now landed on the muddy margin of the pond and began to waddle about, and soon the old birds joined them. But they did not come near the holly.

Suddenly all heads were lifted, fox and duck alike. Something was coming up to the pond, for a stick had cracked. It was some lumbering person who did not care a damn how much noise he made. The mallard sprang into the air, "quacking, quacking," and Rufus heard their voices die away over the wood. The old boar badger came through the bushes, and drank noisily at the pond. Rufus discreetly went over the bank and trotted down through the blackthorn thickets. He left the cover of Coldhangar, and went over the Market Harboro'-Leicester road, heading for Old Poors Gorse.

This was a paradise for foxes; indeed, as far as Rufus was concerned, too much so, as the place was full of them, mostly youngsters of the year. Acres of impenetrable thorn, beloved by the bullfinch and nightingale, and, in season, starred with tender dog-roses and sweet honeysuckle; it was a wilderness of joy. Rare birds, too, were found there, and the red-backed shrike impaled his beetles on the sharp thorns. The great round moon, now no longer red-faced, was clear and bright, and in the hollows, the mist lay like dense white blankets, cutting off cleanly at the base all herbage that was of any height.

Rufus went along at an easy swinging lope, crossing the metals above Lamport station, and stopping for a moment to gaze at the light of the distant signal. In the signal box Robertson was reading the account of a gentleman who had won four thousand pounds in a "penny pool," and his brain reeled at the idea of such wealth. It was cosy in the cabin, and an alarm clock ticked loudly. Below, behind the "Box," he kept his fowls, white leghorns, which were the apple of his eye. He had housed them in an old rabbit hutch, what time he could get some more wood to make them a better home. Rufus, two hundred yards up the line, smelt FOWL, and he came to investigate. The sight of the lighted signal cabin alarmed him, but after watching a while and finding all was still, he came up to the fowl-house.

The smell of fowl was strong and Rufus was very hungry. Moreover, he had missed the duck up in Coldhangar, and he had grown somewhat rash. He began to dig under the wall of the coop, sending the earth back between his legs. Some of the fowls awoke and began to make remarks. Rufus dug on until he could get his head into the hole. The hens began to complain querulously. . . .

Up in the cabin Robertson was nodding by the stove. The paper lay on the floor, and a mouse was eating the canary seed under the hanging cage. The moon shone white on the slated roof of the signal box . . . and down below, something was digging in the inky shadow. Rufus was definitely "getting on." He could now get his shoulders into the hole, between the edge of the wood and the chicken-saturated earth. One final squeeze and he was inside. A second to look round and then. . . . In an instant, pandemonium. Fluttering hens, screams and clucks, white bodies banging and bustling. Rufus seized the nearest hen by the neck, and squeezed under the edge of the wood. The hen proclaimed loudly, and vehemently, and Mr. Robertson heard.

In the corner of the Box he kept a "four-ten," which he used for shooting rats and sparrows that came to raid the chicken run for corn. He seized the gun and rammed a cartridge home, then he flung wide the door. In the moonlight he saw a trail of white feathers leading to the hedge, and something like a brown shadow with a white flapping head was moving by the fence.

BANG! A little cone of red flame jetted against the tarred wall of the signal box, and a singing cloud of lead rattled about Rufus. One pellet stung him on the bottom, and he dropped the fowl and fled up the rails.

Inside the fowl-house there was great to-do, and some of the leghorns were still banging about hysterically. . . .

Rufus followed the railway until he came to the distant signal, then cut across the Draughton fields for Shortwood, still hungry and with injured pride. Passing a flock of sheep, that all bunched and first ran away, and then came trotting after, he went over the wide, rolling fields of Wold. He put up a hare on top of the wolds, but after chasing for a few yards, resumed his trail. A fox will not course his game for any distance. He came to deserted Faxton, the lonely forgotten village in the fields, with its jackdaw-haunted elms and owl-ridden belfry. It lay ghostly in the moon-light, and some black-and-white cattle were rubbing themselves against the posts round the churchyard wall. In a rough, ant-hill-strewn field beyond, he stalked a watchful peewit. This was a great field for them, and in the spring they bred there, but they were very hard to catch. In the moonlight he had not got a chance, and the bird arose "pee-weeing" keenly, and waking others which were encamped among the ant-hills. He entered Old Poors Gorse and hunted it all through without result. But near the hedge he found a rabbit in a snare, partly eaten. This he devoured and, as dawn was greying, he laid up in a dense thicket of blackthorn and went to sleep. . . .

Day had come, and with it a milky mist that bejewelled the spiders' hammocks slung from every twig and leaf. A few robins singing, no other birds greeted the dawn. Up the narrow road that ran across the heath, men were cycling to work. The world was stirring.

In a spider's web slung from the tip of a thorn, from which was suspended a pearl of water, an insect was crying its death-cry. The persistent singing, which was akin to the sound of pig-killing in some curious way, awoke Rufus and he opened his mouth and yawned. The spider came out from the thorns, and fastened on the fly. The shrill singing faltered and stopped. Rufus stood up and shook himself, then he turned round twice and lay down again.

To the east the fires of Corby ironworks died in the dawn.

"Leu in . . . Leu in . . . Leu in." Strange sounds coming across the dew-spangled wilderness of thorn! "Leu in . . . Leu in" . . . "Yoi try! Yoi try!" Rufus raised himself on his haunches listening, listening. His head turned now this way, searching the faint wind, listening . . . listening. Now he looked quickly behind him, ears like fans, nose working. From the distant lane came the sounds of many horses, their hooves rattling on the narrow lane.

Up above, the spider, full fed, retreated to his lair in the thorns.

"Leu in . . . Leu leu, leu in." Sticks cracking, a horse's wicker, commotion, stir. A silent blackbird darted past, scared and swift.

"Leu in, my hearties". . . . "Leu in". . . . Silence, more thrustings in the thorn thickets. Then a long single note of a horn. Silence. Again the long single note. . . . A jay screamed close by and departed over the top of a yellowing may tree. Rufus sat very still. It was the cornfield feeling again, and he did not quite know where to turn or what to do. He could see, under the thick bushes, a stretch of green ride, and as he watched, a fox cub slipped across. A moment later, another, a little lower down. Silence again. . . . "Leu in." . . . Suddenly, a crash of music, hound music. Silence. Again that sound, then a solitary quavering yelp. Then, full cry, all tongues together.

Drawing closer. . . . One more fox, a full-grown dog, came up the path past Rufus and dived into the thick underwood. More hound music, nearer now. Rufus turned round and was off, threading his way between the stems of the spiky thorns. Two bullfinches, a cock and a hen, dipped before him and went into a wall of dog-rose thicket. He flashed over a ride and immediately saw three hounds close to him. . . . Ruby smell. . . . More hound music close behind him. The three hounds, lost in the ride and crying, got his scent and came in after him. But the cover was very thick and they checked and lost him.

Running swiftly, he passed under the thorns until he came to the cross rides. Here he stopped. Sitting a big grey, ten yards down the ride, and just outside the gate, was a man in a pink coat. He had his back to Rufus and the horse's ears were pricked. The man's ears were pricked too, by the set of his head; had he long ears like his horse they would have been cocked forward.

Rufus slipped over the ride and plunged into the thick cover opposite. More hound music and then he had reached the edge of the covert. Out in the field, twenty yards away, another hunt servant was sitting his horse and he saw Rufus the moment he left the cover of the thorns. Behind him he heard the hound music, swelling, faltering, swelling, with it Ruby's voice, though Rufus, of course, did not know that. . . . The young entry, alive for blood. . . .

Rufus slipped off down the ditch. Two minutes behind and the hounds broke cover, a rush of black and tan. Some scrambled over the stake and bound, others tried to get through and became entangled for a moment, shouting, shouting. The main pack was clear of the covert, nose down on the trail of Rufus. Why Rufus? Why Rufus of all the foxes in the covert? The whipper-in raised his hand to his face, the sun catching on the pink of his coat, as brilliant as the berries in the tangled wreckage of the hedge. He galloped to head Rufus, but failed. A great many of the cubs had broken away up wind, but Rufus was heading north-west, towards the open fields and Coldhangar. Behind him floated the sound of the horn—"uuu-uuu-uuu" and faint "view-holloas."

Through a small gate at the side of the covert the field gushed like a stream of black and white water, jostling, pushing and backing. Then, drum of hooves and squeak of leather . . . steady music of the hounds. Along the lane people bicycled furiously and men ran, their coat tails wagging.

T-rump, t-rump, t-rump. Drumming hooves in dew-wet grass, the air like splendid wine. Pamela, on a small chestnut mare, was there, and the wind was in her curls. Hounds were running in the glorious morning. Rufus, unhurried, unflustered, but anxious of eye and with quivering pulses, ran easily. His nightly wanderings had made him what he was, a fit fox, sound of wind and limb, but rather full from his feed on the rabbit.

He emerged through a hedge (a riot of blackberries and red-gold bramble), and found himself in a field of sheep. They were all together in a bunch in the centre of the field, white and clean-looking in the early morning light. Rufus went straight towards them. They scattered and fled, all together, with tossing tails. Then they faced suddenly round and stopped, watching him.

Back in the cover a few of the young entry were trying to find their way out. They could hear the clamour of their brethren decreasing and the bustle of the chase passing away in the pearly morning. They came out on the line, falteringly and puzzled, to be rated by the whipper-in.

After a while the sounds died behind him. The hounds, coming to the sheep-smirched scent were feathering urgently about, striking ever and again a musical clash as the scent came and went. Then Orator, never at fault, picked up the line and led the pack across the danger zone, sure and confident. Soon, full clash again crying all together. Riders, who had grouped restively about at the far end of the field, quickened, and the drum of hooves came again.

Rufus was moving well. The effects of his meal were passing off, and he gloried in the swinging cantering lope that carried him over the dewy grass with such effortless ease.

Two horses were galloping about in the field ahead, wheeling and stopping, and looking over the hedge with working nostrils. Beyond, a bunch of black Angus cattle were moving forward like guards into battle. He ran for them and they ducked, and swung their heads, blowing fog on the cold air in jets and showing the white of their eyes. Below was a little stream, running clear and cold between tufts of rush. He entered it, for it was shallow, and he took a hurried lick at its coldness, and the minnows shot under the shelter of the bank. Running up this some way, he squeezed between two thick thorn roots and found himself in a familiar field where two haystacks stood in one corner. A mass of starlings fled upwards in a burnished cloud before him; and he ran straight over the field and crossed the Foxhall road. It was lying empty in the morning sun, with one listening rabbit standing on hind legs in the grass margin twenty yards away. The sounds of pursuit had died behind him and he slowed down. He even stopped to look behind, but the hounds had faltered at the stream and were casting in the wrong direction.

Orator struck the line for a moment, but lost it again where the starlings had been feeding and gave up at the pistol-shot crack of the whip.

Going gently now with easy loping gait, Rufus crossed the Draughton road and made for Coldhangar and the spreading thickets. The sun was high now and shone with warmth, but its crude light made Rufus uneasy. He must gain the grateful shade of the woods and—secrecy. A goods train was panting up the slope past the distant signal, and Rufus waited until it had passed. Then he went on over the brook where he stopped to lap, for he was a little thirsty, and across the main road below Hopping Hill and its linnets twanging in the gorse. Ten minutes later and he slipped through the gap between the gate post and the hedge, and a jay saw him and swore harshly.

So came to him the first cry of the hounds, a sound that was to become familiar with the years, and which was to become a disturber of dreams.

Pamela turned in up the long drive of Wildwoods. The horse's hooves rustled in the dead leaves of the lime trees, and the gravel was patterned with shadow and speckled pale sunlight.

Her father was shaving, and he came to her room, a razor in one hand and smelling of scented soap.

"Well, Pam, did you do anything?"

"Oh, yes. We killed a brace of cubs in Old Poors Gorse, and one gave us a nice little gallop nearly as far as the Hawking Tower. It was lovely, Daddy. I wish you had come, such a perfectly heavenly morning."

There was a glow in Pamela's cheeks that became her well, and the hint of breakfast in the air was good. When she was changing in her room she looked out of the window at the pale sunlight shining on the bronze chrysanthemums in the border. A drunken Red Admiral was flopping from head to head, and the two white Highlands were rolling over one another on the glistening lawn.

Rufus was left in peace for the next few weeks. The hounds came to Coldhangar one grey morning, but Rufus was not at home. The night before he had gone across to Scaldwell Wood, and, killing meat, had stayed there under the pines all day. When he returned, the rides in Coldhangar were poached by horses' hooves, and there were taints in the air. He found also several hound-droppings by the gate into the covert.

Mr. Brocky and family were a little put out, and did not venture forth for a couple of days. They lay in the earth, sulking and fussing with their bedding, which had to be changed every few days. Besides, winter was coming on and they were getting a little torpid.

Chapter Four
WINTER WOODS

Challenging fox at edge of dark,
Shooting parties in the park,
Clatter of binder, thresher's hum,
A galloping horseman's muffled drum.

SINCE his first experience of hounds in Old Poors Gorse, Rufus took to kennelling in Blueberry Bushes, which were thicker and offered a more secure retreat than Coldhangar. The underwood was nearly impenetrable and grew closer to the ground. Indeed, in some places, a hound would be unable to force his way through. From this kennel he roamed the meadows nightly on his hunting forays, and came to know every gateway, gap and spinney in the district. He was within hunting distance of Talli Ho! and Shortwood, Creaton Covert and Scotland Wood.

Very soon the trees and hedges became stark and bare, and even the reeds of Lamport pools, that were so thick and tangled at the height of summer, seemed to shrink and rot away with the first frosts. And winter set in early that year. At the end of November came the first snow, which transformed the woods and fields into a new and sheeted world wherein the doings of the woodland folk could be read plainly by their imprints. Game became scarce, rabbits were difficult to catch, and Rufus had to fall back on moles and mice for a livelihood, varied (I regret to say) by an occasional chicken from the long-suffering Mr. Jackman on the other side of the valley.

One evening, when the winter dusk was closing in, he slipped out of Blueberry Bushes, and made for Hieaway, three miles away across the railway line. A different place now, unrecognisable from the green fortress of the early summer. The earth where he had been born was tenanted by a badger, a distant relation of old Mr. Brocky, and Rufus did not investigate further, but went up over the pine needles. Under the thick pines the snow was scattered but thinly and lay, speckled greyly, among the needles. The privet bushes seemed much thinner, and only the hollies were warm and cosy. Here no snow could penetrate, and the leaves lay thickly in a scented carpet that made a warm bed. But it was not as cosy as Blueberry, and only a long-nosed gentleman with a barred owl-like plumage seemed to use the hollies habitually as a dormitory. Rufus smelt bird as soon as he came over the rounded top of the hill, and he stalked carefully towards the thick green holly. But the woodcock was away. He had been lying there during the day, quite invisible to the naked eye, and was now grubbing in the little ditch down by the river.

Rufus smelt all about among the leaves, then went up the mound again, under the pines. The night was bitterly cold and very still; up in the pines the wood-pigeons were fluffed out to keep out the frost. Carrion crows were there, too, a whole party of them, for they used the wood as a dormitory during the winter, like many of the other birds in the district. Though rather exposed, it was a favourite wood for all kinds of feathered folk.

Looking upwards among the branches, Rufus suddenly saw two pheasants perched on a thin branch about ten feet up. Their long tails hung down behind and he could see a few frosty stars in the space of sky behind. But they were out of reach, and he could not climb to them. For a long time he sat gazing upwards, and then, perhaps realising the futility of waiting, he went under the pines. He felt a new hunger within him, which was not appeased by meat; a queer longing and a restlessness that made him travel the fields with a hidden impatience, if not a misery. He would frequently stop to listen, and to-night this urge, this hunger, came upon him strongly.

Winter set in early that year

He came out under the gate, and stood in the snowy grass. Over the wide valley and rolling fields lay the very spirit of the hunting shires, bleak but kindly, matter-of-fact. Now they were transformed in the frosty light of the moon in its first quarter, and lay peacefully beautiful, under the arch of wheeling stars. For a full three minutes he stood there listening, the strange hunger within him growing and gnawing.

He slid down the slope of the fields, keeping a straight course for Creaton Covert. He did not stop to hunt by the way because this new fire urged him on, and he turned neither to left nor to right. Now and then he stopped, and stood like a sinister little shadow in the frosty fields. He barked, a short expectorating bark, twice. Silence followed, only a far owl hooted. Above the dark hump of Hieaway a shooting star fell, a streak of light across the blue background, like a white line drawn on a slate, to vanish at the next instant. As he barked he held his muzzle downwards, unlike a dog who raises his muzzle skywards, and the warm breath came in two short jets of steam. He barked again, but still the frosty silences made no reply. Heard from close at hand it sounded, not so much as a bark, but as a gasping cough. Suddenly he heard another fox answering, or rather challenging, and from the sound it must have been in the plover-haunted pastures by the river. And soon yet another, farther away still, from the direction of Creaton Covert.

Rufus waited no longer. He started off at a swinging loping gallop that left a dark line in the snow. He crossed the railway and went through the park of Cottesbrook, with its silent hall glowing from a few upper windows. Stopping now and again to bark, he continued his way, until he reached the wood, and here he sat on his haunches, listening intently. Another fox was barking in the wood and Rufus challenged. The other fox answered.

The hunger within him now drove him to move, and he slipped forward under the fence. Without warning there began a wailing terrible cry, not unlike the sound of the badger in Coldhangar that he had heard when a little cub. It was a hideous sound, and slowly it died away into a quavering shiver. Silence . . . some bird moved uneasily up in the trees. Rufus sat listening, his body on fire with fierce passion. Some farm dogs in Creaton village heard the foxes barking and had begun to bark too, steadily with brazen lungs, until a man went out and thrashed them.

Again that unearthly scream, and Rufus moved forward swiftly through the underbrush. In a clearing sat a vixen, a graceful little lady with velvet black paws. On the other side of the clearing an old fox of some four seasons lay with ears a-cock looking across at his lady love, his jaws slavering slightly. Rufus was across the ride in a flash, his whole being flaming with jealous hate. The sudden gust of passion gave force to his attack, and soon the two foxes were spitting and wrestling like two demons. Over and over they rolled in the snow, biting, snarling, and kicking. Now Rufus was uppermost, now the old fox had him down, and they rolled, kicking and biting, down a little slope. The vixen seemed disinterested, and pretended to catch a flea on her back, but a warm feeling surged within her as she heard the fighting foxes rolling about in the bushes.

Rufus, though in splendid health, was no match for the savage old dog. Yelps of pain rang on the night, and tufts of reddish fur were scattered on the snow. A pheasant, roosting in the holly bushes, could stand it no longer. He flew "cocking" loudly and for an instant startled the two combatants apart. But the heavy dog got a grip on Rufus's neck and shook him savagely until he reeled. Within a few minutes there was no fight left in Rufus, and he slunk down the ride and out of the covert. Miserable and sore he circled the wood. The fires of love still smouldered, and he had smelt the vixen. But he did not dare to challenge again, so he went off miserably for the village.

He tried to dig his way under a hen roost, but had no heart for the job, and when the cocks began to crow in the farmyards he took himself off to his kennel in Blueberry Bushes, hungry for meat and hungry for love.

The next night he was off again. He paid a visit to a garbage heap at the end of a garden, and filled himself with offal which did him no good. But it was food and he was still very hungry. The victorious old dog-fox had gone off with his bride, and Creaton Covert was empty, so Rufus went on over the snowy fields to Coldhangar. Foxes were barking in most of the woods, and the hunger for love carried Rufus for many a frosty mile. There was no vixen in Coldhangar, only another love-lorn fox, a cub from Shortwood. They passed each other with suspicious eyes, but did not fight. Making a circle round Maidwell Dales, Rufus returned to Hieaway, stopping ever and again to call.

As he came up the hill from the little pond where his mother had caught the moor-hen, he suddenly heard a vixen answer from the dark crest of Hieaway. Up under the firs, above the old earth, a young cub was paying court to a vixen. Rufus came on them without either knowing he was there, and for a moment there was a taking stock and a laying back of ears. But the vixen settled matters by slipping off down the slope, followed by the cub, and Rufus was left alone on the hill top. Perhaps he did not bother; his mind was on the little lady with the velvet paws he had smelt in Creaton, and this vixen was, shall we say, a matron; she had already had five families, two in Scotland Wood and three in Walgrave Gorse.

Disconsolate, he hunted up the railway bank, and after a lot of digging, killed a hen belonging to the gate-keeper at the crossing. Then he went back to Blueberry Bushes and a disturbed sleep.

Dawn brought a thaw, and all the trees were dripping and ticking. That afternoon, feeling hungry, he began to hunt earlier than usual, stalking a blackbird that was overturning the wet brown leaves in a ditch. So intent was the bird on its task that Rufus had an easy stalk. The bird was hungry after the frost, and Rufus was hungry too. That night Rufus went again to Creaton Covert to find the little lady who had captured his heart, and not finding her there he went into the country beyond, where he had not been before. But though he met other foxes, he could not find her, and as dawn was greying he came back to Blueberry Bushes.

It was a soft mild morning, and a few song-thrushes were singing, making believe it was spring. They loved to do this, and if a mild day came it was enough to set all the young cocks of the year thinking of love matters—the hollows and ruts in the rides were filled with melting snow, and every spring a torrent of brown water— one might indeed have thought, with the thrushes, that spring was coming. Even the old boar badger and his wife came to the mouth of the sett under the rotted bracken, and sniffed the soft airs. A little after midday Rufus was aroused by a vague uneasiness, and not very long afterwards he saw something coming along under the dense blackthorn. It was a spent fox. The head was hanging, and the jaws were covered with white slime. He was muddied up to the elbows. His brush was dragging along the ground, and a misery of exhaustion showed in the half-closed eyes. Rufus recognised the old dog-fox that had challenged him in Creaton Covert, but he was a very different beast now. In the world of the wild there is no such thing as pity, which is purely a human attribute. And Rufus prepared to do battle.

The spent fox came up to the earth and found Rufus barring the way with fangs bared and ears laid back. Then Rufus sprang like a red flash on his enemy. Just as dogs have their particular enemies, so have foxes, and this dog-fox was hated by Rufus with a deadly hatred. But he was in no mood for fighting now. He had a grimmer fight to wage, the fight for his own precious life. He turned wearily away, and vanished in the dripping underwood. Rufus sat down, looking in the direction he had gone, and began to lick his paws carefully.

Suddenly he heard the cry of the hounds, the sound of the Great Fear. He went down into the earth and lay very still. In a short while the sounds of men and horses came to him. He could feel the vibrations on the earth. The music of the hounds came gradually nearer through the woods until they were all about the earth. There were comings and goings overhead and men's voices. Then the deep notes of Orator and the answering yelps of the pack as they took the line of the spent fox down under the thorn bushes. Rufus lay very still with his nose on his paws, every nerve tense. Soon all was silence again and he stole to the mouth of the earth. The smell of hound and man was appalling and he stopped sniffing the air.

Below the wood there suddenly came on the soft air a tremulously shaking note of a horn, a burst of short sharp notes that floated up between the misty tree aisles. Fierce shouts too and fierce bayings. After a while all was silent, and blackbirds began to chink at the approach of night. When all sound had died away, Rufus stole out of the earth vowing to leave Blueberry Woods for ever. The Great Fear had found him again, and the place reeked. He followed the trail of fox, hound and horse down out of the wood, and on to the misty fields below. At one spot he found trampled grass and scraps of dog-fox fur. Above all, there was the smell of fox blood and he was afraid.

He left the woods and went over the railway. Something drew him to Creaton Covert where his heart had been pierced by the arrow of love, and when the first stars were peeping he called and heard an answer that made him forget the terrors of the past hours. The old fierce hunger was on him again, and his usual caution and sagacity went to the wall. Love lent wings to his feet as he sped silently along under the happy stars.

He came on his beloved under the shadows; but so attractive a young lady was not to be alone. Two other young foxes were there before him, doing battle for her love. But she was disconsolate, mourning for her mate, and she would have none of them. While the cubs were still fighting she slipped away and Rufus followed after.

He followed about thirty yards behind, sniffing the trail, his passions on fire. But the vixen took no heed of him, and she stopped ever and again to call. Then Rufus came up to her, running round her and lying down in the dew with tongue lolling out and wagging his brush like a pleased dog. He would not leave her; but every time he came too near the vixen growled and snapped, and would have none of him. Soon, Rufus, looking back, saw one of the cubs following after, and he whipped round and ran to meet him. Both faced each other for a moment, and then they closed. The sound of the fighting did not interest the vixen, and she went on towards Coldhangar, calling, calling for the mate that would never come back.

The two cubs were evenly matched, though Rufus was the older by three weeks. They fought themselves to a standstill, and lay down panting, with tongues lolling out. Soon the cub got up and tried to slip past Rufus, for he was after the vixen, but Rufus fell upon him again and the battle waged fiercer than before. At last the cub had had enough and he slunk away. Rufus stood his ground and saw him out of sight, then he trailed the vixen to Coldhangar.

She had gone up under the rhododendrons, and out of the spinney on the other side, wheeling left-handed for Blueberry Bushes. He came on her where her mate had been killed by the hounds, and she was sniffing and calling miserably. She ran at Rufus when he approached, and made him retreat a few yards. But he was not to be put off, and when the vixen went back to Creaton Covert, Rufus went too, lying up for the day under the thick bushes close by.

For a week the vixen mourned for her mate with Rufus hanging like a shadow on her tail. He fought two other young foxes that disputed his right, and beat them both. And then one night when the frosty moon was shining from a clear sky, and every gateway and ditch was iron hard with the grip of the cold, a change came to the vixen. Her faithful swain was allowed to come closer and then, with fierce abandon, she took him for her mate. The pent-up fires of love, so long held in check, surged through Rufus when he sensed her surrender. He was on her almost savagely too, and only the muted stars and silver moon looked down on the consummation of his yearning love. It was the great fulfilment of his destiny, the cause for which he was in the world. He did his work thoroughly, for he was clean-run, fit dog-fox.

Rufus and his wife kennelled for the next few weeks in Creaton Covert. At night they hunted together under star and cloud. The long frost held, and the cry of the hounds was no more in the land, and though game was scarce, those were happy, happy nights. No longer was there the aching torture of something lost in the dark woods. All life was in tune; therefore, it was good. Animals do not experience love in the manner of human beings, though some foolish people seem to think they do. It is, with them, a deep hunger, deeper than any mere physical hunger of the stomach, and when that hunger has been appeased there comes contentment and peace.

Up in Coldhangar the little woodland pool was frozen over with thick black ice, and the foxes wondered why they could not lap. They licked the slimy surface and tried to walk upon it, but their pads could get no grip when they moved faster than a walk, and were apt to shoot from under them in an alarming degree. But the bitter cold weakened many of the woodland creatures, and as Mr. Brocky did not approve of the cold, there was more to be found in the woods. In the ash poles the pigeons huddled nightly, their crops filled with frosted greens. This killed many of them, and they would drop from their perches and provide excellent fare for Rufus and his wife. One day, in the woods, the vixen found a dead tree stump, with a hollow in the top amongst the ivy. She smelt "bird" within, and with the help of her mate they began excavations. The wood was rotten and came away without difficulty. Soon the vixen put in her head and withdrew it. In her jaws was a little wren, dead with the cold. Rufus also explored the stump and found six others inside. They had huddled thus for warmth, but their wee bodies had succumbed to the cold. As animals know no sentiment, this pathetic little band, which had perished as gallantly as any polar party, was devoured without more ado.

But there was better game in the woods. The mallards still visited the pond and the prolonged frost had made them weak. One evening, Rufus, coming up the bank with his usual caution, saw three standing miserably on the ice. As he lay watching them another circled round and joined them, skating seven yards before it could stop. After a fruitless stalk the mallard rose, all save one duck which was too weak to fly. She scrambled, quacking loudly, under the holly bushes, and Rufus nailed the squawking bird at the foot of the smooth green holly bole. He took it up to the earth under the rhododendrons and shared it amicably with his wife.

The chickens at Jackman's farm were barricaded in at nights, and nothing short of blasting operations would have effected an entrance, though both foxes spent several nights trying to dig under the hen-house.

The frost still held. Pamela, with cheeks (and, I venture to say, nose) as red as a wild rosebud, skated happily with her skylarking friends on the big lake below the house. These skating parties lasted long into the night and some bright spirits hung coloured lanterns round the pool, and they waltzed on the ice until the early hours. Rufus and his wife watched suspiciously from under the hanging spinney on the hill, and did not approve.

With the continued severe winter, game became scarcer every day. It was chancy work relying on weakened birds and animals, and all the rabbits by Blueberry had been ferreted and shot by the farmer. Old Zank the heron was reduced to a mere bundle of bones and feathers on stilts. Rufus saw him often, huddled by the side of the stream waiting philosophically for the frogs or fish. But even the swift water was soon running under arches of crusted ice, and the poor fish-eating birds became weaker every day. The kingfishers that built in the sandy bank by the crossing ash spinney were on the verge of starvation, and one night the vixen found one, a flame of shot blue, lying stiff and stark on the shingle below the high sandy bank. Up above was his favourite perch, a dead willow branch. Here he used to sit in the summer heats, when the gnats were weaving over the cattle-scented water, and catch the silver minnows. The vixen ate him, but found him very fishy. Still, it was meat, and she ate him, bones and all. Only his long bill she left on the shingle, the weapon whereby he had caught many a good fish for his wife and family. A wandering crow spied it and carried it three fields away where he lit on a fence and pecked it. Then he dropped it and it fell into the bottom of the hedge, sticking down between the stout horizontal branches that had been laid by the woodcutter's bill-hook. A mouse found it there, but could do nothing with it, and that was the end of that.

The foxes became so bold that they began to hunt during the day, and both Rufus and his wife began to slim a little more than was healthy.

Old Zank, the heron, was fishing the ditch below Henton's farm. This spring had never dried up since the world began, almost. For hundreds of years it had flowed down between the fold of the meadow from where it bubbled up among its cresses by the field gate. Two yards from Zank's legs a snipe was probing the half-frozen ooze and his long bill was plunged deeply into the mud feeling for little living things with his sensitive soft beak-tip. Zank's eye seemed more fierce than ever as he sat hunched among the reeds, with the cold, cold water running between his toes. He saw the snipe, but did not move. Game came to him, not he to game, and he pretended to be a rotten tree. If the snipe had come within reach of his bill I could not answer for what Zank might have done. Though he caught fish and frogs and worms, he was partial to anything that looked good to eat, and he might have had a shot at eating the snipe. But the latter little gentleman knew how to look after himself, and he kept out of reach. In the frozen grass a flock of starlings were waddling and quarrelling, sometimes fighting one with the other in jealous greed. Poor things, they were starving too, and they worked so hard.

Over the hedge, Rufus, hunting alone, had heard the bicker of the birds as they waddled in the field. He slipped through the hedge and went down between the rusty stalks of the willow herb and peeped out. Just in front of him stood Mr. Zank, deep in meditation and the problems of life. Rufus was for an instant a little taken aback. This bird was so big he could see under his tail, and as he stood deliberating, the heron shifted his feet and began to stalk slowly down towards the snipe, his long neck moving forwards with each stride, and his spear of a bill couched in readiness. With the movement Rufus smelt him, and it was a warm smell of food.

He slipped along between the bank and the rusty stems of willow herb, and when the heron stopped again, Rufus stopped too. Something had made him suspicious, and now his neck was stretched right up as he scanned the surrounding fields with his baleful eye. The snipe suddenly shot up with a little tearing sound, and at that moment Zank launched too, taking a step or two forward to get himself off the ground. Rufus saw his meal escaping under his very nose and leapt, like a red flash. He caught the heron just above the thigh joint and there followed a terrible struggle. The huge wings were spread, and threshed like a swan's, and so powerful was the uplift of them that Rufus was flung about. He hung on, waiting for a split second in which to shift his grip. The heron was using his bill, too, a terrible weapon, but he was handicapped by the fact that the fox was close beneath his body.

There was something very grim in that battle. Had Rufus got a lower grip, and had the heron been fighting fit, the fox might have got the worst of it, but as things were the odds were in favour of Rufus. The crystal drops of water were scattered this way and that, and the heron's neck was wriggling like an eel, trying to spear downwards. Then he screamed, a terrible harsh scream, and in that moment Rufus shifted his grip. The great wings flapped convulsively twice and lay still, spread like a grey and black cloak over the snarling fox. But the clear water was running half over Zank's head and the beautiful baleful eye was dimming in death.

Rufus took the dead bird by the body and lugged it up the bank. A heron looks larger than it really is and poor Zank was very thin. Rufus tried to pull him through the hedge, but he stuck; so the fox ate half the bird, where it lay in the rusty weeds. That night he brought his vixen down to finish it off, but there was nothing left save the legs and beak. Round about, on the spring's margin, was a strong smell of strange fox, and obviously somebody else had been there. So they went off together through a flurry of falling snow to Lamport village. At the top of the rectory garden the gardener had dumped some waste from the house, potato peelings and odd scraps. The starlings had been quarrelling over it all day, but there were still some tasty morsels left, including a large marrow bone.

Having fed, they went across the snowy park to Scaldwell Wood and kennelled under the warm firs. Below the wood was a large square pond full of big pike and moor-hens. The latter, as soon as the frost had turned the water into a sheet of plate glass, had taken to roosting in the woods, perching in the ash poles, like pigeons. There were more rabbits in Scaldwell Wood than at Coldhangar, so Rufus and his wife decided to stay there for a while, until the frost lifted.

Chapter Five
THE NEW YEAR

Sound of bells from the village spires,
Bringing a new year to the shires;
Patter and tick of the summer rain,
Making the woodlands sweet again.

WOOD ANEMONE

NEW Year's Eve . . . the sound of many bells abroad the quiet shires, growing and dying over the night-scented pastures! Rufus and his wife, hunting the cold shoulder of the Faxton fields, heard them, the bell voices in the starlit night.

Oh Man! Man! what sentiment he finds in the voices of the bells! The sound is mixed with all his greater moments; in birth, in mating, in death, in joy and in sorrow, he rings the bells. In many a grave, grey tower the sweating rustics manned the ropes, their shadows big and bobbing in the lantern light. But with a greater sanity, Rufus and his wife slipped over the sweet grass, alone together under the arch of stars. . . .

The frost had eased at last, and over the ice on the little ponds there lay a film of gummy water. The earth was sticky too, clinging to the foxes' pads and to the hobnails of the rustics as they went about the boggy gateways. Pamela had abandoned her skates and was praying for the mild weather to drive away the frost for good. Skating, dancing, shows in Town had begun to pall. She longed for the covert side and the music of the hounds that had been silent for so long. Her greatest joy lay in the swinging gallops over the wide fields, sound of the horn on the winter airs, and the pink bobbing coats. She hunted, not because it was "the thing," but because she loved the countryside and horses, and the thrill of clearing an "oxer" was the greatest thrill of all. When hounds killed their fox she contrived to be a field distant, for she could not rid her mind of the little big-eared cub slipping away in the twilight of a summer night.

Monday, hounds were meeting at Brixworth . . . could it really be true! Ruby had done well at the Puppy Show, and was shaping splendidly; some said one day she would outmatch even Orator in wisdom!

She went out to the stables and communed with Wendy, her little mare, whispering into her ear the great news. Monday! Monday! Wendy, mumbling an apple in her velvet prickly lips, blinked foolishly and tossed her head.

Rufus and his wife spent New Year's Day under the firs in Scaldwell spinney, and listened to the dripping trees. In the evening four hundred and thirty-two wood-pigeons came in to roost, and their clapperings awoke in Rufus vague memories of Hieaway and March evenings. . . . Some mallard and a single teal had come to the pool in the dusk, but swam well in mid-water, and Rufus could only watch them furtively from the cover of the whitethorn. He caught a moor-hen, though, that was over-confident and bold after the frost, and this he shared with his vixen under the firs. That night he hunted in Shortwood, but neither the vixen nor Rufus killed game. . . . Hounds did not come to Scaldwell spinney until two o'clock in the afternoon. Holcot spinney had provided a fox which had been lost after a tiresome hunt to Old Poors Gorse, where Rufus first heard the music of the hounds and knew the Great Fear. . . .

The fox and his vixen were asleep under the warm firs, curled up like two tired dogs with their noses in their brushes. The vixen awoke first and sat for a while listening intently. Then Rufus awoke and together they sat on their haunches, listening, listening. A lot of horses were coming over the park, and by the little hand gate in the wall they waited in a compact throng of pink, black and white. A horse wickered and the vixen got to her feet. The Huntsman was bringing his hounds into covert in fine style, and watchful sentinels had been posted before the foxes had begun to move. The vixen went down towards the wall that ran alongside the wood, and leapt lightfooted and lithe on to the top of the stones. Rufus went down to the pool, and slipping along the foot of the mound, left the spinney by the north corner. Here he was seen by the whipper-in, who "halloed" him away.

Hounds had separated and were feathering through the firs. Orator picked up the scent of Rufus and led his pack down the bank, but four couples got on the line of the vixen and jumped the wall. By now Orator was nose down, and the music crashed out in lovely discords as the racing black and tan hounds spoke to the scent. Up the side of the wood came the pistol shot of a whip, and the excited hounds were turned after the others. They needed little turning, however, for they had heard the deep tones of Orator. Rufus slipped along the headland and crossed the road by Jackman's farm, heading for Old Poors Gorse, but he had no intention of going there. He had in his mind where he wanted to go, and was unflurried and cool.

Across from the hand gate in the park wall, the field was streaming in a torrent of colour and with mighty drum of hooves. Some jumped the low wall on to the headland; the majority divided in two streams for the gate in either corner. These gates dammed up the field as a dam holds a torrent, but in a few moments there was not a horse in sight. Only two excited boys ran along the road, and five cyclists, the light of battle in their eyes, pedalled furiously towards Wold.

Back in Scaldwell spinney all was quiet again, save for a swearing jay, and the trees seemed to be brushing the soft breeze through their branches, as much as to say "Phew! Glad that's over!"

The vixen ran swiftly to Walgrave Gorse; then, finding she was not followed, lay down in its prickly fastnesses to wait for night.

Rufus was running for his life, his bright happy life. Shortwood was left behind, and he had failed to check them there. They had carried his line right through the underwood without a falter, and were hard on his heels, singing happily. Over the rolling fields the horses were thundering "fullump, fullump, fullump!" Rufus crossed the road just behind a stationary car. Two men were standing on the edge of the road; they had their backs to Rufus and were looking the other way, so they did not see him. He followed the headland across to a little ash spinney, and went on down into the soft grey valley. Some rooks, feeding in a field of winter wheat, saw him and followed, stooping at him with discordant cries, but he sped on. Dead ahead lay Blue Covert, a thorny barricade, boggy underfoot, and he slipped in under. His tongue was hanging just a little, and his legs were muddied, but he was not rattled—yet. . . . There was a big drain in the ditch on the far side of the cover; to this he ran, entering swiftly like a weasel. But after crouching in the tunnel for a moment (the light at the other end glaring like a great eye), he backed out again and went up the ditch.

Some magpies had seen him and were swearing, flying from branch to branch and cocking their cunning heads sideways at his slinking form. He decided to leave the cover and went on down to the railway and the brook. There, in some thick reeds by a little pond he lay down, listening. . . . Hounds came to Blue Covert after a short check on some foiled land where the rooks had been. Soon they were swarming through the covert like bees, and the field was grouped on the hill behind. On the neck of Pamela's mare was a smear of froth, one on each side where the reins had touched. . . . Orator came to the drain and bayed loudly. The terrier man dismounted and realised how nice it was to be on his legs after the gallop. . . . The Huntsman had made a cast beyond the drain and up the ditch, but hounds somehow seemed uncertain, and for once Orator appeared definite that Rufus was in the long tunnel of the drain. But when the terrier came out the other side and shook himself, they thought Rufus was behind them, under the thick cover. The afternoon was closing, and in the

Watchful sentinels had been posted

valley the distant signal winked a red eye at Rufus. But he lay where he was in the reeds.

It was Orator who redeemed himself. He picked up the line where Rufus had crossed the winter sward, so sweet-smelling now in the dusk. In a moment all was movement again. The field sorted itself out, a smaller field now, for the faint hearts had tired of waiting and were jogging back to the Draughton road, clattering in a gossiping cavalcade down the street, where the white-aproned village women watched them go past. Rufus heard the hounds again, and the fear leapt within him like a warm anguish.

He slipped over the rails and crossed the stream, going up the slope to Hopping Hill. He waited for a car to whiz by, and then crossed into the gorse, heading for Coldhangar. His mouth was hanging open and his head hung low, and he was muddied and very tired. Perhaps, though I don't think so, he remembered the beaten fox that came pleading for life to Coldhangar, but he was not beaten yet. Beyond the gorse he crossed some cold plough, and it was this that saved his life, this and the merciful winter dusk. Hounds took the line at a screaming pace over the railway, checked at Hopping Hill, faltered in the gorse, and lost him on the plough. Had the afternoon been an hour earlier Rufus would have been a beautiful machine no longer. . . .

Hounds were called off after a short check on the plough, and went jogging back in the darkling to Brixworth, tired, muddy and content. . . .

In the early hours Rufus came back to Scaldwell to find his mate. She was not there, only the reek of hounds. He found her in Walgrave Gorse. Together they trotted away through the mild night, and by dawn were hearing the first thrushes singing in Hieaway Wood. Rufus was still very muddy, and it took him most of two hours to lick himself clean. Then he and his mate went down to the rough pasture by the crossing spinney, and killed a rabbit by the stream. The hounds were not to bother them again for many days: the world was still beautiful. Happy huntings, mild days, and the swelling chorus of hopeful birds: and his wife was uneasy with hunger; a new hunger, strange, beautiful; the loveliest hunger in the whole wide world. . . .

She chose as her nursery a dry warm earth in Blueberry Bushes, and a puzzled unhappy Rufus tried to be helpful but was snapped at for his pains. He used to go off in a huff and hunt miserably until dawn. He also, I regret to say, had some scandalous affairs with a vamping vixen in Coldhangar, but we will not pry too far into his private concerns.

The evenings were lengthening and a new promise was abroad in the quiet shires, the little sheltered meadows plaintive with infant lambs. Rufus would take his vixen to Hieaway some evenings, and the old owl perhaps smiled to see them under the pines. It had been a hard winter, but he had weathered through, and begot another family in the hollow touchwood oak, his tree by right of inheritance from a long line of grave and courtly owls. His wife was sitting her three rough eggs, and he brought her mice with a certain self-righteous air, like a Victorian gentleman of the old school. A bit of a hypocrite, too, perhaps—but we are not concerned with his story now.

March was here, shouting March, the Merry Monarch of the Months. He set the fir trees tossing with boisterous glee, and made the ash poles rock until they shrieked for mercy under his rude and merry jests. He brushed and garnished the woodlands and the fields, and made them ready for the new fresh harvest as he had done for a million years. And from out of the blue oceans of sky where cloud got short shrift, the first chiff-chaff came into the welcome shelter of the budding thorns, to rest after his passage over the sea. Hesitatingly at first, he sang, as though he were apologetic, and to this halting music Rufus's first children were born.

Some days before their birthday, the vixen ceased to hunt, and Rufus did the nightly foraging, as became a solicitous husband. And, after the five mole-coloured babies arrived, Rufus continued to supply his family, different indeed from his father. In all fairness to the latter, however, it must be remembered that a litter of February cubs does not get the same paternal attention as a March litter, so the old gentleman cannot be too sorely blamed—we will not slander the dead.

The blind babies, sucking helplessly at her teats, sent a creeping thrill of pleasure through their beautiful slim mother. Soon, too, she could hunt again, and it seemed as if a load were lifted from her body. The noses of the little cubs were pink, though they soon darkened. At fourteen days they began to see dim lights coming to their growing brains. Their eyes did not open equally, and at seventeen days the most backward of the litter still had one eye completely closed, which gave him a very sly expression. As the colour of their coats changed to brown (the brown appearing first in streaks on the head) their baby blue eyes changed to amber. The vixen began to sleep away from her babies, but was ever at hand to protect and suckle when the occasion required.

Rufus, now that the vixen hunted too for game, became less solicitous, and began hunting forays unaccompanied by his wife. Indeed, they now chose to hunt apart every night, and game was fairly plentiful so that the cubs throve exceedingly. Every evening now they came and played round the mouth of the earth, just as their father had played in the long ago. One bright morning the willow warblers were filling the woodland with their gentle scales of music, for they had come in during the night. They hopped about among the immature leaves that were opening in the sheltered places, seeming like tender buds themselves in their greenish-sulphur hues. And soon a whitethroat was chattering like a mountain beck outside the earth, in the whitethorn bushes. He sang in a chuckling hurry, as though he must be done with his song, full of the exuberance of life. He told the cubs what a beautiful world was in store for them (the silly bird knew nothing of hunting and bitter winter famines), and he showed them in the bubbling vigour of his song how the dog-roses would soon be cascading in a pink and white waterfall down the high hedges. The willow warblers sang to them of the tender opening of little green things and of life born anew. And the cubs sat about the mouth of the earth, listening with all their ears. Then, as children get restive under adult amusement, they would tumble and play about the dead leaves, and with the exercise their little bodies gained strength and stature.

Soon the first cuckoo came shouting through the woods. The call arrested the cubs at play; so unbirdlike a sound was puzzling and they listened intently. So he had come down the long, long centuries, with his clean spring music, and the while man fought and struggled and loved and hated in his own very little world of which he thought so much. But the cuckoo was older than man even, like the badger and the stoat, knowing only the simple things, the sunshine and the wind, the ripple of the summer breeze over the mowing fields, and the hot sun of light-drenched lands, far over the sea.

And then, one evening that was very still, when sturdy lambs were proclaiming from the green pastures, a nightingale came to the whitethorn. His lovely mellow notes startled the woodland into a reverent silence, and proud of his powers he sang to the cubs with exultant beauty. His song was a maturer song than any of the other birds, and he sang, not of green baby things and the opening of life, but of the beauty of woodland cloisters where no man comes; of mossy badger-haunted rides and summer glory, and the cool recesses of the inmost fastnesses of whitethorn. He sang thus about this England that he loved because he had never seen her in her old age. It was to him a land that was ever young, like a maiden that never grows old.

With all this promise of good things the cubs frisked and played in great high spirits, knowing perhaps, too, that in the bosky shadows, a lithe and loving mother was ever ready to lay down her life for their sakes, and the world was good.

Mr. Brocky was very spry in Coldhangar. For all his years

A nightingale came to the whitethorn

(and they were many), he moved with surprising agility, and rheumatics had not yet touched him with insinuating stabs. In the mossy runs he knew so well he hunted nightly, and went grubbing about happily in his green and secret kingdom of thicket and ride. He did not confine his activities to Coldhangar, but wandered far afield under the spring stars, visiting Maidwell Dales (where he found a dead pike) and the blackthorn snow of Blueberry Bushes perfumed the hours.

In the spreading crowns of the green thorns, close to the earth, a cock bullfinch was bowing and posturing before his lady love. Blowing out his chest as pink as a rose petal, he whistled his low love whistle, turning himself this way and that before the duller-coloured hen. She was beautifully plumaged too, with the exquisite restraint of Nature, and the softer, more subtle greys and blacks of her plumage seemed a perfect foil to her brightly plumaged mate. Suddenly she raised her Roman nose skywards, drawing back her head and quivering her wings in an ecstasy of love passion. The cock scrambled on her back, and for a moment there was a little fluttering of wings as he served her. Then he hopped off on to a twig, and bowed and postured, overwhelmed with the fires of love. The hen shook herself, and almost, shall we say, put her hat straight, and then flew "witting" away through the bushes. The cock thought a moment, cocked a full eye after the fleeing white rump, and followed. In the crown of the whitethorn a few thin fibres had been cunningly woven, and when he got there his spouse was busy, treading and turning in the diaphanous cup of roots.

Mr. Brocky came up the bank, heavily, and blowing a little like the old gentleman that he was. The cubs, playing with the skull of a weasel at the entrance of the earth, heard him and in a moment the cavern of the entrance was yawning darkly. Mr. Brocky came up under the bushes and smelt round the leaves and moss. Then he smelt the weasel's skull, and stood a moment in meditation, turning his head hedgehog-wise and looking over his shoulder. Against the shadows of the thicket his black-and-white face sang out vividly, and there was something a little sinister in the piggy eyes and striped head. All was very quiet in the woods. Not a jay screamed. Even the evening thrushes had ceased their vespers. The bullfinch and his mate were collecting nesting material on the outskirts of the wood, and there was no sign of a vixen anywhere. Mr. Brocky went slowly into the earth like an old gentleman going down into a subway in the street. . . .

When the vixen came over the bank with a baby rabbit in her jaws she immediately smelt the badger, and she dropped the rabbit. The hair began to rise along her back, and her lips curled back into a snarl. She went swiftly to the earth, and met Mr. Brocky coming out, the white stripes on his head smirched and dyed with blood. The old gentleman was not a pretty sight. The vixen was on him in a fearless rush of savagery, and so violent was her onslaught that the badger turned back into the earth, the worst move he could possibly have made under the circumstances.

The earth was an enlarged rabbit burry that Rufus and his wife had made themselves, but as Mr. Brocky was a large person there was not very much room within the hole. In fact, there was not enough room to turn round, and behind him was the incensed mother. And she used her jaws for all she was worth, making the badger kick out behind him with his long claws. The vixen was strong and her jaws were strong, and her gleaming ivories sank deep into his stern. The vixen, her mask covered in blood, worried and savaged silently, and the knowledge of her loss lent a maniacal fury to her strength. Once outside the hole the badger was able to turn and use his wicked jaws, but the vixen danced round him like a boxer on her toes.

He rushed at her, with swiftness for so large a beast, and drove her slowly backwards down the slope. His back leg had been bitten to the bone, and he was leaving a stream of blood all down the bank. Then something was on him from behind. A deep anguish passed through his neck as Rufus's teeth met below the long fur. Now both foxes were on him and the three fighting creatures rolled under the whitethorn. Rufus knew his old enemy, and he had a score to pay, and he fought silently and with swift parrying bites of his jaws.

The badger by now had had enough. This was the first time in his life he had been beaten, and he was getting weak from loss of blood. He backed through the bushes, swearing and snorting, trying to keep the foxes at bay. But they fought him right out of the whitethorn to the edge of the ride. Here he managed to cripple the vixen with a deep crunching bite in her off foreleg, and the strength of the bite splintered the bone. The vixen slunk limping up the bank, and the fox followed her.

As for Mr. Brocky, he took himself off slowly for Coldhangar, and feeling weak from loss of blood, and the agony in his rear, he lay down under the wild rose bushes on the edge of the wood. Then, with a certain dogged courage that had preserved his race from extinction, he made his way back to Coldhangar, and reached his sett just as the owls were thinking of bed. For many days he was not seen on his nightly wanderings by the woodland people, and perhaps he had died.

When the vixen entered the earth, dragging herself painfully, she found a shambles. In her agony she lay and mourned, the dog-fox with her. But, strange to say, one cub had survived. When Mr. Brocky had come up the bank the cub had been some way from the earth, hunting on his own among the leaves, and playing with little sticks. He saw the badger go into the earth and had followed curiously. He had even tentatively entered, but what he saw and heard made him flee to the cover of the bushes on the top of the bank. He had watched with wide-eyed terror the battle on the bank, and was too frightened to come back, even though he had seen his mother enter the hole. When the cub saw Rufus it ran down to meet him, and tried to feel for teats that were not there. The fox pushed him to the mouth of the earth, and the mourning, wounded mother dragged herself out.

To say that joy was in her eyes would be untrue, for animals do not experience the same feeling and emotions as man. But the yearning aching sense of loss vanished, and she licked his little mousey coat delightedly and gave him herself to suck, lying at the mouth of the earth upon her side. That night, she carried the cub to a little spinney of ash trees by the railway, and feeling too weak and sore to go farther, kennelled there with him under the dog-rose bushes. As for Rufus, he went off by himself, glad to be rid of the smell of blood and death. . . .

The vixen under the wild rose bushes was in throbbing, burning pain. The bite of the badger is the worst possible bite. Its jaws are so closely articulated (the lower jaws are hinged securely to the skull and work in deep grooves) that they cannot be dislocated. And all that day she lay in throbbing pain, getting no sleep, and worried by her teasing cub that gave her no peace. She was forced at length to leave it, and lie up under the close-cropped railway hedge.

The whitethroats bubbled in the briars, and on the little weedy pond a moor-hen "cruiked" loudly.

That night she carried the cub to Coldhangar, the home of Mr. Brocky, and every step of the journey was a burning, shooting agony. . . .

Rufus was digging out a rabbit's nest by Wildwood pool. He did not dig in the mouth of the hole, but directly above the nest. His nose told him where the babies were. He dug a neat round hole straight downwards, and it was hard work. He stopped now and then to rest, looking about him with sly eyes. As it was not yet dark, his eyes appeared as slits that gave him rather a sinister appearance.

In Wildwood pool a pike jumped, among the weeds and close inshore, and at the splash a moor-hen complained from the reeds. In the wood the wild hyacinth made a sea of heavenly blue, echoing the sky among the bases of the trees.

Rufus dug on, and soon reached the nest. He ate three rabbit babies on the spot, and carried the remaining one into the wood and buried it under the wild hyacinths. When he had gone away across the park, the doe rabbit hopped out of the wood and across the damp grass, ears pricked and with frequent stops. She smelt fox and was suspicious. When she came to the earth scattered about and the round hole above her nest, she smelt round delicately. Little bits of blue fur lay in the grass, and there was the tiny hind pad of one of her babies lying by a cow platter. She sniffed it long and went away unhappily, back to the dark mass of the wood.

A white barn owl came past on silent wings, and went beating up the hill, her round, mothy eyes searching the grass below her. In the far distance, the cur, by the barrel up at Jackman's farm, barked to the stars, "wow, wow, wow, wow... ow!"

Chapter Six
SUMMER HUNTINGS

Scent of the bluebells, mouldering logs,
The tangled rush of snipey bogs,
Smell of a vixen ripe for cub,
Of a roosting bird in the laurel shrub.

RUFUS was now a fine specimen of a fox, though not yet in his prime. He measured three feet nine inches over all, from the tip of his nose to the end of his brush. The latter was still without a white tag, though a few white hairs grew there. To look at him, an uneducated person would have taken him for a vixen, and so he was described by a man who had seen him about his huntings in the evenings. He was not above rolling in badness when he felt inclined, though he did this more in the spring of the year when sexual passions warmed him.

He was now hunting almost exclusively on his own, the vixen likewise. The latter limped from her encounter with the badger, for her forepaw was almost useless. Nature had done its best with gristle and tendon, but could not heal the crushed bone, and she was unable to travel far o'nights. Consequently, she fell into the habit of raiding farmyards, and was seen by Mr. Jackman, junior, one evening, down by the stream. She was carrying a runner duck, and her guilt was established. Moreover, the evening was windy and there was no one to see, so the double-barrel spoke twice (the first shot was a clumsy one and gave an agony that is too fearful to describe), the second shot brought merciful oblivion.

The skin adorned Mrs. Jackman when she went to market. A local taxidermist had dyed it cunningly, and the fur was long and fine. . . .

The son of Rufus, now able to fend for himself, did not need her help, for he had learnt how to catch beetles and was busy with his apprenticeship, just as his father had been in cubhood days. . . .

Rufus had found a hedgepig in Coldhangar. He met it coming down a woodland path and it had rolled up at his approach and was now defying all efforts of Rufus to unroll and be eaten. After pricking his nose very badly on the pied spines, Rufus went off a little way and lay down watching it. All was very quiet in the woods for it was late evening. The air was heavy with summer scents and blossoms, and in this scented paradise the nightingale was singing to his mate as she brooded the five olive eggs in the ground ivy. The minutes passed, but still the hedgehog remained stubbornly in a ball, a round spot of darkness on the dim-lighted woodland path. Then, after an age, its head and snout slowly came up from beneath it, and it looked about. Rufus, lying under the dark bushes, made no move. His head was on his paws and he lay stretched out as if dead. Only the ears were cocked intently.

Finding all was quiet, the hedgepig suddenly began to run, very quickly, like an old lady trying to catch a bus. Its little black legs took it over the ground at a great pace, and smoothly as if it were running on castors. It went under the thorns, towards the wood pool, where Rufus caught the mallard on the ice. Rufus followed swiftly like a shadow, and just above the pool he ran at it, but it flicked into a ball again and lay half hidden in the nettles. Again began the waiting game, Rufus going away a little distance and watching. The smell of the hedgepig exasperated him and made his mouth dribble.

The hedgehog began to unroll again (after a long while in which an owl hooted), but a little stick, dislodged from the oak above by a skipping grey squirrel, rustled the grass close by its snout, and it rolled up with a jerk. Once again it unrolled and began to trot along the top of the bank. Rufus was on it again.

With a short, dabbing hook of his paw he rolled the little beast over on its back. Below was the pond and Rufus patted the hedgepig again with his paw, turning it over in the grass. Several dead leaves, relic of autumn days, were impaled on the spines. He patted it again and the round ball, gathering momentum on the slope, rolled with a splash into the water.

The widening rings shivered the shadows and went crinkling under the spreading darkness of the holly. Once in the water the little beast could keep in a ball no longer, and though it was not above its back, it had fallen in upside down. So it was forced to unroll with a little piggy sneeze, trying to cough the beads of water from its lungs. Rufus went in after it, and nipped it across the snout. Then he carried it painfully up the bank and cleaned out the inside, leaving only the jacket behind. It was delicious. . . .

The bluebells turned brown and withered, only the juicy green stalks remained on the woodland floor. In the low whitethorn were numerous nests, bullfinches, garden-warblers (who plagued Rufus with their alarm, "U-wit, U-wit," whenever he came near); and in the long grass by the side of the wood, willow-warblers and wood-wrens. Rufus caught a great many of the latter, smelling the nest so cunningly hidden in the long grass and catching the little sulphur mother before she flew out. Partridge nests, too, he found, and fed upon, and a few pheasants, though the latter birds were scarce in Blueberry.

In a great bush of wild rose a bullfinch had her nest and within were four baby birds twelve days old. They had not the black cap of their parents, and their breasts were sparrow-brown, but the white spot was above the tail, and the wings blue-black and barred. The white spot was useful, for the bullfinch is a woodland bird, and this white spot acts as a beacon which a mate can follow in and out of the secret fastnesses of the woods. It served the same purpose as the moor-hens' undertail coverts in the reed forests, or the white tail of the deer. . . . They were nearly ready to fly, crouching, tails to centre, in the flimsy cup of roots.

Rufus, coming along the mosses, smelt the droppings under the nest, and looking up, saw the little structure just above him. By standing on his hind legs and putting his front paws on the thorny tree he could just reach the nest, and he began to do so, ears a-cock. But at the first movement, the fledglings burst from the nest like a bomb. Three could just fly a little way, but the weakly one fell directly down on the moss, where Rufus quickly bolted it. The movement was so instantaneous one could scarcely follow it. He now turned his attention to the others. One of them, a cock, sat on a honeysuckle stalk, bending this way and that to keep his balance. But his little pink baby claws were weak for want of gripping practice, and he fell down, fluttering wildly and with a little pipe, into the thicker cover of the honeysuckle. Here Rufus pounced this way and that, when he heard a movement, but he lost it. When he looked for the others they were nowhere to be found.

The two parent birds now came up, and piped urgently in the thickets, but the babies were too wise to reply. Only when Rufus had gone away did they begin their monotonous, deep pipe, that carried for a long way in the warm woods.

One day, when Rufus was day-hunting, in the afternoon, he saw a ring of rooks grouped in a parliament close to a hedge. A stoat was running from one bird to the other, but the rooks simply hopped a few yards and swore at the lithe, brown snake of a creature. Rufus went over to see about it, and the stoat ran down a mole hole. Then the rooks turned their unwelcome attentions to Rufus. . . .

He became adept at catching moles, and in the evening, when the shadows began to steal in long cool lines down the slope of the hill, and the cattle got up heavily, one by one, and went over to the gate in the corner, he would watch for the moles working, which they did with great regularity. One scoop of his paw in the heaving, red earth and he had the mole out on the grass, burrowing wildly, with wrinkled human hands, hands like those of some old labourer who had spent all his life in horny toil. But mostly he shunned the day, and in the summer heats would be sleeping under the thorns of Coldhangar, or the remote thickets of Old Poors Gorse. Out in the hot fields the cattle would run with lifted tails, as the gads pierced their hides with needles of pain, but Rufus was in the cool, cool woods, dreaming away the sunny hours. . . .

Halcyon days when hunting was good, and the woods secret, beautiful with scent and bird-song. Nobody ever came to Coldhangar until the autumn, when village boys would explore for wild nuts, so it is small wonder Rufus liked the place so well.

He grieved a while for his lost mate, but it did not wound him deeply. The fires of sexual passion belonged to the winter months, and there was nothing to trouble him now and he waxed large and stout with good living. And how pleasant it was to lie, listening to the low surf of wind breaking on the reef of firs in Hieaway, and sniff the scent of turpentiny trees!

Old Poors Gorse was lovely too, with its curtains of dog-rose and dark wildernesses of thorn, where nothing larger than a fox might walk. This place was as deserted as Coldhangar in the summertime, because even birds-nesting small boys could not face the thorn, and that is saying a lot. But it had not the peace of Coldhangar, with its shadow-banded rides and nightingales, nor the austere beauty of Hieaway with its eternal surf of wind. Moreover, Old Poors Gorse was infested with magpies and their prying eyes were everywhere. Did they but as much catch sight of a red form slinking under the bushes, they would let the whole world know of the fact, and brazen it abroad, the ragged flying sneaks! And that blue rascal, the jay, the cause of many a fox's downfall when hounds were running, he, too, was just as bad, and the fortresses of blackthorn were ideal for breeding.

With the passing weeks the summer reached its full maturity. One morning Rufus awoke to find all the fields alive with young starlings. They seemed everywhere, in the hedgerows and meadows, and even in Coldhangar itself. The rich "cheurring" call was insistent as they clamoured after their burnished parents. It was the week when all the starling babies leave their nests up and down the country. From gable and parkland elm, from old woodpeckers' holes, from farmstead roof and barn, the new tide of young blood was abroad, making the meadows musical with their cries for food.

In Coldhangar the ring-doves sat their flimsy nests like grey jugs, looking stupidly out of their mild, beautiful eyes at the woodland greenery above and below. When scared they would leave with such violence the white eggs would sometimes fall to the moss, and Rufus had many a meal in this way. The turtle-dove, too, bred in Coldhangar (exquisite creature, like a Japanese print), but it loved the denser thickets best, in Old Poors Gorse. All through the summer heats its drowsy lullaby rocked the nocturnal hunters to sleep, "Cruuuuru, Cruuuru, Cruuru," almost a purr of contentment.

In one of the tall ash trees at the top of the wood, a sparrow-hawk had adapted an old carrion crow's nest. The four young hawks were nearly ready to fly, splendid fierce-eyed creatures, who looked with scornful eyes on their fierce mother. Her curious cry, a wickering yelp, was a familiar sound in the daytime as she swept silent and watchful through the trees. It would rouse Rufus from his noon-day nap, and cause him to sit on his haunches, gazing with baleful slits of eyes and ears straining. . . .

July came once more to woodland and meadow, and with its coming the birds fell silent. In the tips of the oaks, young green leaves appeared, as though a second spring was on the way, and in the brakes, the blackberry flower clustered whitely. To these blossoms came the White Admiral, prince of butterflies, floating down the green rides with a flight more beautiful than any other British butterfly. Big tawny fritillaries flitted, too, in the chequered sunlight, with silver-studded wing. Once, Rufus came upon a dead rabbit, stinking with advanced decay, and upon it was a magnificent butterfly, opening and shutting its wings, as it fed on the meaty juices. It was a Purple Emperor, rightly named, though his tastes belied him. These midland shires were the last stronghold of the butterfly, and when he was not feeding on some putrid carrion, he sailed in more majestic pursuits round the oak crowns of the forest.

The true insect of Coldhangar was the Speckled Wood, and this butterfly was ever to be seen when the sun shone, taking his exercise in the chequered shade.

Where the misty pink spires of the willow-herb stood in a tangled forest, there was a big wood-pile (ash poles cut long ago for fencing, and never, for some reason, used). In this wood-pile, and beside it, lived long grass snakes, evil-smelling, raspy creatures, though harmless in all truth. When the weather was hot Rufus would see them swimming in the wood pool, swimming gracefully and with wagging ease. He killed one once, but the smell turned him and he left it where it lay, in the willow-herb jungles.

One little creature of the woodland which Rufus could never catch was the red squirrel. There were a few still left in Coldhangar, though they were fast dying out. They would sit and scold from the high branches and pass rude remarks when they saw Rufus slipping over the green mosses. The grey squirrel he sometimes caught, stalking them behind the boles of the trees as they skipped about in the lush grass.

Out in the mowing grass the reapers got busy, and new scents filled the evening airs. The yellow plates of alder blossom turned into plum red berries, rich harvest for the autumn birds, and the mountain ash, on the edge of Coldhangar, began to blush its round full berries also. The son of Rufus had gone to kennel in Talli Ho! Rufus came on him some nights while hunting mice in the gloaming. But they took little notice of one another, and the cub was considering himself quite grown up.

Cubs that have been transferred from their original birthplace when only a few weeks old are more liable to develop a wandering habit and, therefore, when cub-hunting begins, they are not so likely to be killed. Some of the fox cub families that had never travelled far from their original wood were apt to stay at home, and like man himself, this meant they were narrow-minded and with a narrow outlook. Travel broadens the mind, even for an animal, and this was one of the reasons why Rufus had survived.

After a wet July, August came flaming in, and the woods in the valley became so hot and lifeless that Rufus took to sleeping outside, in the top of a hollow willow tree that grew by the midge-haunted brook. It was cool by the water, though the flies bothered him, causing his ears to twitch in his sleep. Though the tree was nearly perpendicular, Rufus could climb it with ease, for ivy had embraced the rough trunk and the hairy coils of strangling root afforded an easy step-ladder.

When the sun was molten at midday, the cattle, red-brown, mild-eyed beasts, smelling of buttercups and grass, came and stood knee-deep in the stream, swishing their tails to keep away the flies. The sucking noises they made when they withdrew their feet from the clay sometimes disturbed Rufus. Then he would peer down at them from between the ivy leaves, a sinister slit-eyed mask.

And sometimes he could see jack, basking on the surface, slowly oaring with barred fins. Incautious roach, venturing from the shelter of water-daisy and waving cress, would be scattered in whirl of water and the jack would go off, the silver body held cross-wise in his shoe-shaped jaws, shaking it as a dog shakes a rat. All this Rufus would watch, when he was not sleeping.

One evening, young Jackman, with a gun under his arm, came along the brook in search of some unwary rabbit out for its evening feed. He had his wire-haired terrier with him, a famous dog for rat-catching, and the little beast smelt Rufus up in the pollard. It danced round the foot of the tree barking so much that the cattle came up, running and blowing, in a body. But young Jackman could not be bothered to climb the tree and he contented himself with throwing up clods of earth, red, dry earth, that burst on impact and rattled down in fine dust on to the trembling body of Rufus. But the fox, hearing no scrambling hobnails on the bark of the tree, lay where he was and kept mum. After a while the barking ceased and Rufus heard the fellow go away down the bank of the stream. Not very long after there was a shot from the direction of the mill, where a rabbit was kicking its last in the browned buttercups.

This experience was docketed in Rufus's brain. "Lie still, and don't move."

Swallows used to skim the dun-coloured water, and the white-rumped martins gathered mud on the edge of the stream. It was an interesting place to sleep. Occasionally a blackbird or finch would see him in his bed and scream it aloud to the world, and once, two mistle-thrushes made his life a burden for a full hour.

Then, with early September, the mornings became chilly, and the sun lost its old power. So Rufus took himself off to Cold-hangar again, and kennelled there until the October moon.

Chapter Seven
THE TRAGEDY OF THE ICE

*Tang of the cow-pats in the meads,
Withered smell of the winter reeds,
Smell of the mushrooms, crushed by hoof,
Old swallows' nests in the shippen roof.*

JUST as to a child, one day seems like a week, so to a wild animal a day is like a month. Rufus came to be aware that he was immortal, that life would go on for ever; beautiful, changing, and full of adventure and interest. With this new autumn, he had grown wise and grave. Every night he was learning something new and experience survived meant more knowledge and confidence in himself.

Like any other thing that lives and has its being—trees, grass, animals and men—he was subjected to the laws of Nature and circumstance. And the ever-changing, moving particles of mobile existence so ordered themselves, or so fell out, that he survived many a narrow shave. The difference of a split second might have meant his exit from this bright paradise he knew, but still he held the cards of fortune and felt the warm blood pumping in his arteries.

Now that twitch fires burnt in the fields, filling the autumn landscape with blue incense, and flame in leaf and fern told of another winter on the land, he felt a restlessness for long huntings by wood and hill, in lands he did not know. The tide of high summer had receded, leaving a strewn and scented foreshore, where the wrack and jetsam of greenery scattered. That mysterious wave of life, drawn back by the feebling sun, as the waves are attracted by the moon, was ebbing fast.

From the cottage gardens arose bonfire reeks, and the late-brooded martins had at last reached some decision in their roof-ridge parliaments and were no longer in the soft and scented land that knew their birth. To take their place, the "chuck, chucking" fieldfares came, in high-flying flocks from the dark pine woods of the Northlands, and sometimes, as he roamed the starlit pastures by the Hawking Tower, High Headlands, Darnel, and Marrow Down, he heard the wild geese ghost-hounds, passing high in the night for the mudflats of the Wash. At those stirring sounds he would stop and listen, moved (who knows?) more strongly than even Man himself, by the wild passage of far-flying hosts.

The fresh harvest of fox cubs were tried in the fire by the Young Entry, and many foolish ones perished in those magic-misted mornings when the sun struggled with the pearly vapours for mastery. A few wise cubs survived, and among them the son of Rufus, his first-born. Rufus, with happy fortune, contrived to go unhunted and unseen, and after a little while, the rusting wilderness of Coldhangar knew him no more. . . .

He had found a new retreat in Summermoon, part of the great forest that once covered half the county almost, and in these noble forest lands he lived content and happy. Deer were there, he often saw them, and many knotty oaks, that had seen gayly clad nobles perspiring with the chase. Pheasants were there, too, and they formed a larger item in his bill of fare than hitherto. The long-nosed woodcocks came in one frosty night, and he killed two of them before dawn, under the hollies where they had dropped asleep, dead tired after long journeyings.

Here he was to see the long, creaking tumbrils, bearing the fallen giants of the forest down the rutted rides, as a giant is borne to his last resting-place, moving as slowly as any funeral cortege down the crowded streets of reverent trees. He would hear the echoing clap of the woodman's axe and the titanic splintering bang of a toppling tree. In the forest the hazels ripened, to be gathered by the forgetful squirrel, and harvested by the careful mice, and in the old blackbirds' and thrushes' nests the dormice stored their pips and stones until these garners overflowed.

Sinister, wicked fungi glowed and flamed in the rotting decay of stumps, and from the blackberry bushes Rufus helped himself to a rich harvest, for the berries scoured him and made him clean.

Apple trees in cottage gardens were stripped of their bending weight of red-flushed fruit, and the low hum of the threshing engines seemed like the deeper tones of some great symphony of thankful praise. . . .

November came, softly and clad in white vapour that transformed the hills and valleys with mystery, and the woodlands talked their drip-talk through the lengthening nights. And all that month Rufus went unhurried and unharmed, shunning the ways of men and man-made things, living the life he loved so well.

And then December, who had done with all misty nonsense, and let folk feel his manly sting and bite. The last leaves wavered down and the trees took on their purple hues and madder blues. The frosts came nightly, and the snow, whitening again the land where once the bluebell grew, and turning men's minds to purity and peace. The holly berries shone from the dark, varnished leaves, and home-going woodmen cut some branches against the merry Yuletide.

Pamela, older now, and with an added freshness, saw these things and noted them. She lived on the sunny side of the wall, and knew not many evil things; she was at peace in this world of clean winter airs. With a largeness of mind that became her well did she grasp and seize the elemental things, the simple joys that know no ageing or decay. To be across her mare and to feel the wind of speed surging in her ears; to listen (not without a pang) to the sorrowing weep of the horn by the covert side, those were to her the greatest delights.

Was there ever such a Christmas as this! Snow, real snow, holly and mistletoe, and the voices of happy bells in the snowy night. Carollers with lanterns and untuneful voices tramped the snowy lanes. Rufus, hunting across from Summermoon to Badby, heard them and saw their distant bobbing lights make a fairyland of the snow. And Rufus, perhaps feeling or catching the spirit of the happy time of feasting and adventure, raided Brownlee's farm-yard and captured with commendable stealth, a great, pink-wattled gobbler for his Christmas dinner, mighty feat of strength and daring under the crusted dome of stars. Brownlee tracked him over two fields into Badby Woods and vowed fearful vengeance with trap, gun, and potion. . . .

New Year's Eve again, and frosty bells, dancing and feasting in hall and grange, jollity and mirth. Under the wooden floors and beneath flagged parlours, the trembling mice wondered what was toward—there was so much dancing and merriment. And far from the scenes of these heated merry-makings Rufus was hunting, with the old hunger upon him, some slim young vixen with velvet paws.

He had come from Summermoon, a point of several miles, into the nakedness of Badby Woods, all lovely in the starlight with delicate twig tracery. The frost was weakening and the snow had gone, but in the woodland pools the ice was still thick. Down the dark aisles he went, stopping to bark in the solemn quiet, sniffing and listening the midnight airs. The woods were full of foxes, cubs, and a few old ones, and some of the latter Rufus fought and beat. But he could find no lady for his favours, and when the dawn came he went to ground by a badger sett, close to a fallen elm that sprawled head first down a bank. . . .

Daventry was all astir that January morning to see the brave meeting of the hounds. Many an urchin there, still bilious from the yuletide board, many a sturdy burgher and his spouse, well-clad against the winter chill. And what a brave company the Field, in pink and black and spotless white! What running of feet and clopping of hooves; what laughter, what beauty, what wealth. Lords and Ladies, knights and esquires, fortunate folk

Living the life he loved so well

on whom fortune smiles. Some were there to be looked at, some to see, some because it was "the thing," some for the joy of the horses. Some were there for the joy of a hound, a few for a pretty face. Some were kind and some were cruel, some knew sorrow and others mirth, some were poor and some rich, some had blue blood, some black, all were there in a clattering throng. But the first whipper-in was missing.

They moved away from the town on the hill, trailed by the camp followers on cycles and foot, a road full of colour, and life, and noise. They flowed like a slow stream, filling its bed from side to side, from lip to lip, and they thinned out soon and the trots rang out. The foot folk were left behind and only the fortunate and fair rode out to the draw in Badby Woods, where Rufus lay, curled right round with his nose in his brush....

A jay, screaming, awoke Rufus. And he knew in a quiet little pang, the Great Fear. Hounds in every ride, the squelch of sucking draw as a horse pulled his feet out of boggy ride. It was a time to be going and not for tarrying. He left his kennel and slipped away, slowly, stopping again to look back and listen, his eyes puzzling slits in the grey morning, a paw upraised, like a dancer's toe. Then there was hound music through the trees and the weep of a horn, "Yoi try! yoi try! ... Heu in, my hearties, yoi try!" Paddings of feet and crashing underwood.

Rufus was puzzled. Hounds were on a fox somewhere, yet he was aware of others, mute, near the fallen tree where he had lain. There was cracking of whips and a lot of angry shouting, and then behind him the hounds speaking to his scent. The bitch pack had divided, and there was a bit of a jam. The Huntsman, unflurried, did his best, but the absence of his first whipper-in was like the loss of a limb to him. Rufus went leisurely, stopping ever and again, ambling on; the hounds puzzling, now mute and feathering, now moving and speaking as they caught his trail. Two jays went screaming, and frightened rabbits ran past him, some stopping like Rufus and looking back at the noises behind them. Far away the rest of the pack were speaking, and a few lost hounds crying to be found or to find.

He slipped out of the woods and found the coast clear before him, only a man, in the far distance, running away from him through the trees, a stick in his hand and shouting. Rufus made for Fawsley Park and its lovely trees and house. Over the red beech leaves he went, loping, loping, looking back; through a holly spinney, under an iron railing where a wren scolded. Down across the yellowed grass where moor-hens scurried for the upper lake, and seven mallard took swift wing and circled over the purpled park, a noble park, and noble trees. Two men, wood-cutters, saw, and shouted and ran, they knew not why or where, but aimlessly towards him with some queer hope of heading him off and doing him to death. A gamekeeper saw him and lost him, making for the frozen lake. Out in the middle the ice was thin, thin because of the aristocratic white ships of swans that cruised so disdainfully beyond its slender floes. More duck rose as Rufus came to the edge of the ice, and moor-hens fled for the grateful cover of tall, slender reeds (where the rotting cups of the reed warblers were still slung like little baskets from the yellow rods).

He went straight out over the ice; why? Did he know what he was doing, could he guess the tragic sequel? No, I do not think so.

He crossed the thin ice, broke through with one slender paw despite his feather-lissom weight, and then turned left for the firmer ice. He gained the far shore and went up the park, past the storied house watching from its graceful windows above level lawns. He crossed an open space, disturbing seventeen portly, blue wood-pigeons, who clappered round and all lit in the top of an oak to whose upper branch brave brown leaves still clung, making a mockery of winter. Then more woodland, then a road where an old man was leaning on his spade, listening to the music of the hounds. He did not see Rufus, for the latter went up a ditch and crossed the leaf-strewn road twenty yards above him, still leisurely, still listening, still looking back. . . .

Down past the wood-cutters streamed the hounds, not a rider in view as yet, oblivious of everything but the scent. Sterns together, black and tan, a brave sight. The wood-cutters stood silent now, and saw them dive into the holly spinney.

And now came the huntsmen, riding, riding, and behind the broken medley of the thundering field. More riders, more drumming of hooves. Down over the cold grass, long and tangled and dead winter-yellow, went the hounds: Picture, Diamond, Gayly, Rivulet, Raiment, Rosemary, Sybil, Stately, Mermaid (alas, poor Mermaid, what mockery in your name), Risky (alas, how true), these and more, racing over the winter sward to the frozen pool.

They are going now, over the ice, past the droppings of the mallard, white splashes on the ice, and now the outraged swans take threshing wing, necks nodding and "hoosh hoosh" of mighty pinions. Blind with the fury of the chase, skidding on the ice, still speaking (rarely now) to the taint of Rufus, first goes Diamond to her doom, then Rivulet and Rosemary together, the firm surface crumbling and wheezing under their feet. There goes Raiment, swimming, grunting; Sybil, Mermaid and Picture. Now Gayly, now Risky and Stately. They swim across the black, cold water to the far thin edge. The others spread out around and feather up among the yellow reeds where the ice looks firm and bubbled-black. Forepaws clamber, reaching for a hold; cracking wheeze of paper-thin ice. Grunting, swimming, twenty legs working, running in icy deep that gives no grip.

Now men urging, loved voices calling, "Come back, Rosemary," "Up here, Diamond." . . . Men running on the ice, some going slowly, fearfully, as the pistol-shot cracks star and splinter. "Fetch a ladder you, run quickly or we'll lose the bloody lot!" "Do something, can't you, don't stand there!" Horses on the bank, pink coats, black coats, some dismounted running, shouting. Here come the wood-cutters over the beech leaves, "Gone through the ice, can't get out." . . .

The thin ice breaking at every scramble, sterns slipping back into the waters of death. The pigeons are up from the oak tree and fly swiftly northwards; the sight is not to be borne.

Diamond gasps and goes under; Mermaid too, slips down and reappears. Hound cries of terror, watery, pitiful; feebling leg strokes. Rivulet's under. . . . Scared pike, darting under the black roof of ice at all this pother, see a slow drowned body drifting downwards, then another, feebly turning as the black tides of unconsciousness shut like a blanket on trembling senses, down, down, down, down into the darkness and never waking cold. . . .

Rufus, three miles away, was scratching behind his ear. There were no sounds behind him now, and the soft mists of the thaw smelt appetisingly good. . . .

A dog fox (not Rufus) night hunting once in Fawsley Park, came upon a stone that smelt new. Man smell, too, round about, and trampled earth. He cocked his leg against the stone. On its face were graven the names of

Picture	Diamond
Risky	Stately
Sybil	Gayly
Rosemary	Mermaid
Raiment	Rivulet

Chapter Eight
ALARMS AND EXCURSIONS

*A world of sounds both faint and far
That tell where the love-lorn vixens are;
Rustle of wood mouse, rabbit's thump
As he beats his pad on the grey ash stump.*

LITTLE was seen of Rufus in the days following the tragedy of the ice. The barking of dogs by keepers' lodges told sometimes of his passing, and angry masters would bellow for silence from mullioned window. The farm dogs heard him sometimes, too; Willow Tree Farm on its windy hill heard him passing; but all the shouting cur could see was the high, riding moon and the tossing of bare branches in the shadow. The cackling poultry told of the secret travels, and sometimes a trail of white or brown feathers blowing in the cold grass showed the way he had gone.

Leadhills Farm, by the slow stream (bare fringed now with rotted sedges) heard him, barking for his love in the silences of the small hours. And the farmer, lying awake by his warm wife's side, heard the lonely barking in the night. But all he could see was the moonlit stack-yard and a large rat running along the wall. Then his feet got cold and he went back to his muttering wife and he muttered too; he had suffered long with the little red rascals. Watchers by cottage bedsides heard him, and blear-eyed doctors sometimes heard. The Rector's son, cramming for Cambridge, heard him, in the silent Rectory of Hinton Hine.

Only those whose work is of the night sometimes heard him. Bellamy Bill, the Woodhall poacher, as he set his snare by the five-barred gate of Little Deene Close; the village constable, stamping his feet by the frosty turnpike, heard him; a little boy, six years old, wakeful with the measles fever (down in the cottage at the end of Willoughby lane), and he was afraid and cried.

And who saw Rufus? The white owl, of course, silent of wing and with eyes that burned; the upland hare, hopping on the moonlit plough; the sheep, folded within hurdles on Tinton Hill, and many other night folk, furred and feathered, saw him (some of them saw him in the last fleeting agony of life), but no man saw him.

And all this time, Rufus, hunting nightly far and wide, came to know his country with an intimate knowledge. Unlike man, who can see over a wide range when on his flat feet, the fox's vision is limited, for he is close to the ground. The only chance of a wide view is when he climbs a tree or steep slope, or when he is on an upland ridge. For the most part his view is bounded by a close horizon, a straggling bullfinch or oxer, an edge of red, rich plough. He knows his country by the hedgerow gaps and drains, by gateways and winding stream, by lane and road, by fallen tree or sarsen stone. But once traversed, a field is known, and that knowledge remains and is preserved.

After much searching, for he was hard to please, he found him a mate, a year older than himself, a wise big vixen who had known three other dogs before him. She had also known the Great Fear and had come to scorn it. Happy at last in sexual matters, Rufus hunted anew with greater energy, and one February night took his vixen away from Badby, and set his mask for the old haunts he knew so well. . . .

Rufus was raiding a hen-house by Lamport station cottages. He had sniffed round the signal cabin, but the white leghorns were well barricaded. Besides, the red sparks shooting from the iron chimney scared him and made him nervous. Those wandering points of light belching from the nether pit of Robertson's stove seemed strange stars, shooting, then wandering against the velvet

Little was seen of Rufus

pall of night and suddenly vanishing. He had burrowed under the wire netting where the rains had rusted it, and the task of getting under the wooden wall was easy, the caked asphalt, child's play. He pinned his hen, a tough old bird and a blameless matron, by the body, and carried her (shrieking wildly) into the field. He did not stop to kill her, but went away across the meadow towards Lamport pools. Mrs. Valent heard the din and awoke her husband. Together they padded to the window in their flannel night-shirts, and opening wide the sash heard the dying screams going away up the fold of the hill.

Next morning Mr. Valent hooked out an old rat trap with rusty, ugly jaws, and after a little sandpaper and oil had got it into working order, set it by the hole in the wire. Rufus, bold at his former success, came the following night for another hen; a silly thing to do, but he was rash. When he came near the shadowy house at five minutes to one, he was startled by something close to the wire. Mr. Valent's fine Persian cat was couched in the hollow he had dug, her ears flexed back and eyes green with hate. Her forepaw was fast in the iron jaws, and the rat she had been chasing when she was caught was safe in a drain-pipe under the chicken house.

Rufus eyed the cat and the cat eyed Rufus. Rufus smelt chicken and he was not afraid of anybody but Man and the Great Fear. He sprang on the cat and received a deep gash from a lightning rip of her free claw. She also seemed to explode in a splitting bomb of fur. But Rufus, infuriated by the sting of the claws, bit deeply into the cat's neck and killed her. She lay moaning and twitching, paralysed, the whole of the time Rufus was in the hen-house, selecting another victim.

In the morning, Mr. Valent, going on duty, went to visit his trap and found the cat. He took it in to Mrs. Valent, and she put her apron over her head and wept loudly and long, for she was fond of the cat. . . .

Two nights later Rufus came again, and found a piece of rabbit meat lying just inside the wire. But it smelt of man, and he sniffed it carefully, the hair creeping on his back. There was also another smell that reminded him in some vague way of his mother, so he left the meat where it lay and slunk away up the line. And Rufus lived.

Twice in the next fortnight he heard the cry of the hounds, and saw bobbing horsemen over the edge of a green hill, but he was left in peace.

When March was in, he went with his vixen to Coldhangar, for she was thinking of a family and the cubs were stirring within. And it was to Coldhangar came the Great Fear, one windy morning when the trees were restless, and the ash poles creaked and clattered under the caress of the wind. . . .

Low-flying birds, wide-eyed and scolding, gave him the first creep of uneasiness. Then a "cocking" pheasant, bustling down the ride with tail held off the ground, running like a stag. Then a jay, the foxes' enemy and friend, tearing his harsh voice in the thickets. The vixen, heavy with young, was in the earth, and Rufus left her there and went up slowly under the rhododendrons. It was a bad scenting day and Rufus knew it. He did not hurry himself, and when he reached the edge of the wood he stopped to yawn like a dog. This might have been taken for boredom, but it was really excitement, just as a dog will yawn. His mouth opened so wide he gave the appearance of laughing, and his eyes, screwed against the daylight, were mere slits of bright cunning. He slipped between two twisted roots, through a rabbit run, and out into the field.

The second whipper-in, like an equestrian statue in pink and white, was sitting his horse twenty yards above Rufus when he broke cover, and he let him reach the far hedge on the hillside, before becoming galvanised into life. Within five minutes hounds were coming through the hedge, nosing the sward and speaking at intervals in an uncertain manner. But they got his line up the ditch and raced the hill. Round the corner of the ash poles gushed the field, taking the stake and bound with graceful ease, all save a portly gentleman on a grey whose experience of hunting was of short duration. He executed a neat parabola and sat, surprised, with his hat over his ears, while the grey did not tarry, but fled into the distance, stirrups jumping and swinging, and reins a-dangle.

Muddied, angry, and running foolishly, the portly gentleman followed, grasping his hat in one hand and his crop in the other, wishing with all his heart he was sitting in his office with the muffled roar of the Strand in his ears. Pamela, taking the same fence, saw his plight and took pity. She caught the grey by the far hedge and brought it back to the angry man, biting a trembling lip that betrayed the humour brimming in her grey eyes. It was decent of Pamela because the music of the hounds was going down into the misty dingles below Hazelbeech. . . .

Two men were ferreting rabbits in the burrows of Parson's Piece. They heard the thrumming of hooves and the cry of hounds, and climbed on top of the laid ash branches in the hedge to get a better view. The white terrier and a lean greyhound with them stood with pricked ears, their hind legs trembling.

Rufus came through the hedge into Parson's Piece slowly, springing the ditch with a graceful ease. The two men saw him at once and mouthed strange sounds, and one took off his cap and waved it wildly. The two dogs saw Rufus, too, and went tearing down the side of the hedge, greyhound leaving terrier far behind. Rufus saw them coming and went like a red bolt down the ditch, the greyhound gaining. He slipped back again through the hedge on the same side as the hounds. But the pack went straight over the hedge where he had slipped under. One, Outcry, caught for an instant by the tangled branches, hung, clawing wildly with back feet to get a grip. Another, Captain, fell head over heels and rolled into the red water at the bottom of the ditch. Here the foil of the cur dogs brought them to a check, and they feathered about all over the field, oblivious of the urging rustics. The Huntsman, coming up, turf flying behind him in muddied tufts, and with gobbets of lather on his horse's bit, brought his wide-eyed restive steed to a backing standstill, and ignoring the rustics' directions (as was his habit) decided to cast beyond the hedge.

Rufus, having shaken off the greyhound by slipping through the hedge, went on down to Barrett's spinney, a little ash plantation in the valley. Its hedge of red beech leaves looked like rusted iron. He entered by a rabbit run and went straight through the spinney into a cow byre. Out again, under a gate, past a derelict harrow half hidden by weeds, disturbing a covey of partridges that fled whirring over the far hedge. On, across a green meadow and a stubble field, and then right-handed for Naseby and its slender spire. . . .

He passed below the village, and a woman carrying a bucket saw him. He went on down to the reservoir and entered the reeds at the upper end. Here he lay down and waited. . . .

Hounds, picking up the trail to the cow byre, were feathering all about, silently and with waving sterns. The foil of the manure-sodden straw drowned the scent, and they knew not which way the fox had gone. The Huntsman, making a wide cast to the far hedge, could not get hounds to speak, and some thought the fox must be hiding in the byre.

Then Captain, questing on his own along the stubble field headland, caught a whiff of scent and gave a little whimper that brought the others to his side. Soon they were hunting slowly over the stubble, speaking very occasionally, as though unsure of their minds. The second whipper-in rode on ahead and saw the woman with the bucket, waving a handkerchief. And so the hounds came on down to the reservoir, slowly but surely, with an occasional short burst of music.

Obviously Rufus had gone to the reeds, and the stream of hounds and horse came down the green slope of the valley. Naseby village was alive with the sound of hooves, and heads peered over dimity curtains. . . .

Rufus heard them coming and went slowly on, past the head of the reservoir and over the Welford road. Here he doubled back and ran down the road for thirty yards into a ploughed field, where sable rooks were nodding after worms. They saw him and rose in a cloud, stooping and wheeling. But the birds were hidden from the Huntsman by the rise of the hill, and when the hounds came up to the road the rooks had drifted away like blown leaves. Cars came to a standstill and people stood up in the seats, peering, gabbling and gaping. The road became a river of waving sterns and horsemen, but they lost the scent there. It was the final check, and Rufus, still going slowly and stopping to listen, heard the sound of the horn and shots of whip dying away into the distance.

So he went on slowly back to Blueberry Bushes, and when dusk was muffling the fields, returned for his vixen in Coldhangar. He found she was out hunting, so he went off to look for her, catching a mole in the Willow Bottoms, en route. It was a windy night, and all the branches were chattering and talking. Round the lambing-folds by the Manor Farm he found some offal, and there was his vixen too, pleased to greet him and to be caressed. Soon she would hunt no longer, for her days were shortly to be accomplished.

They left the lambing-fold before dawn, and went back to Coldhangar. Finding the taint of hound was worrying, they kennelled in Hieaway, and did not return to their former haunt until the following night. Five days later Rufus's second family saw the light, and the task of feeding it fell upon his shoulders.

As for the Great Fear, it did not come to Hieaway again that spring, and Rufus and his wife were left in peace. . . .

One night the vixen went down through the rolling fields to

the water meadows and followed the railway along to Brampton links. She found a round white ball in the thick furze and carried it back for her babies to play with, for they had reached the stage when they enjoyed a romp of ball. The next night she went again and found two more; these she carried in her mouth back to the earth, and the babies enjoyed their games hugely. The balls were found by an earth-stopper the following season, and the tale went round the Hunt. Cheap jokes were made by golfing enthusiasts as to where the lost balls went, but that was inevitable.

In the oaks of the crossing spinney the rooks were busy all day long, flying to and from the fields with sticks in their bills. Soon, in the wool cups, the first green black-spattered eggs were laid, and the sounds of the excited birds brought spring again to the land. By the winding brook that ran through the spinney a wild duck made her nest under a bramble, where the grass grew long and lush before its time, and throughout the gentle April days she brooded her great green eggs, half hidden in the down from her breast. She listened to the rooks calling in the tree tops overhead, and the chuckle of the friendly stream was ever in her ears as it went talking round a little willow, singing for very joy that Life had come again. She lay very still, invisible to the sharpest eyes, and once, when birds-nesting boys came through the wood, she took wing, long before they had reached the nest and circled low over the hedges. The boys saw her. "Coo, there's a dook!" But they passed the nest by under the bramble.

Beneath the oak trees lay broken eggshells, and the dead leaves were white with droppings. Rufus used to come and smell around some nights, on the look-out for young rooks that had fallen out of the nests, but he never found the duck's nest. Perhaps a kindly Providence was watchful. One day, the first egg chipped (it was a lovely warm day when the floor of the spinney was white with anemones and gay with primroses) and during the night the others hatched. The mother duck took her little downy babies along the stream as soon as they could walk, and that night Rufus, scavenging for rooklings, found the empty downy nest and was interested. He was so interested that he searched the stream down for thirty yards and then did not bother. That was lucky, because the duck had taken her little ones up the brook, and so they were spared.

A water-rat that lived under the bank where a great root bulged, and the kingfishers sometimes came, also investigated the nest, but next morning a heron caught it, otherwise it would have eaten two of the ducklings . . . but there are no IFS. . . .

All those ducklings throve and grew, guarded by a fearless and brave mother, and when autumn came with strange new urges they took swift wing one night, and went to a place where no man ever came, but that is another story. Those brave mothers of the wild, how brave, indeed, they are. For them no reward and plaudits from the multitude, no brass bands and speeches. Yet wild life (and Life, too, if we but knew) has little use for pity; it knows no shadow of mercy and is absolutely heartless. Therefore, life can go on; waste there is of life, but to live at all there must be a very big margin of matter, and a field of grass or a seashore can humble man. Humble him, because he judges everything by his own standards, and measures everything by himself. And so it is a green meadow can humble him more than the starry heavens, if he will but use his brain. And then, being humbled, let him use that reason that makes him aware he is humbled, that warfare and cruelty might no longer be in the land. . . .

Sometimes Rufus would watch the birds flying high in the blue ceiling of the sky, but he did not realise how clogged were his feet, or how free those wheeling atoms seemed to reasoning Man. He lived in the mystic hour when the woods were silent; and in the great wonders his senses told him, his nose, his ears, and his eyes. His chief concern was food, and how next to fill his belly, for only Man is privileged to reason, ill though he may use that privilege. Rufus had his loves, but these were mere hungers, soon remedied and stayed. He was part of the great machine of existence, but he found his part to be good. So close to the heart of life, he understood its inmost secrets well, and lived more fully than many a man or woman. He knew the fear of Death, but understood not what Death might be and formed no wild dreams of survival afterwards. . . .

And so through all that summer he hunted happily his well-loved haunts. He saw the grey heron stalking the mole-hills in the early mornings, before man or the sun were out of bed, and started to see the blue bolt of a kingfisher shrilly piping down the mazy stream. He found a tree-pipit's nest in the crossing spinney, and ate the hen and the eggs, and they were good. And in the late June evenings, he would wander happily along the brook side, looking for mussels in the mud, and they were good, too. Of the bright day he knew little, for he slept away the sunlit hours; his lot was of the night and the million pricking stars. Then did his life's blood course to the full, and by the passing minutes, he approached the prime of his life, to when his feet were fleetest, and his senses keyed to the perfect tune. He came to the full-budded rose, to the last inch of the forest oak, to the final ear of perfected corn. . . .

Once, in the late evening, Rufus was eating a mussel by the bend in the stream where a great root lay in the midgy water, and where the dace were rising after the flies. And it was there he saw his first otter, slipping like a great vole along the far bank. His ears pricked as he watched it, and his brush twitched until it glided out of sight. When later he heard a human-sounding whistle down the misty brook, he was afraid, and went away over the fields, looking back and scenting the air.

In Coldhangar, Mr. Brocky hunted his old rides and trod his well-worn paths. He did not feel the scar on his rump, save in the wet weather, but like an old gentleman, he grew testy and morose. Moreover, his teeth were not what they were; but he had grown to a great size. He left the cubs alone in their earth, for some reason best known to himself. Perhaps his nerve was broken and he would never eat baby foxes again. But still, you never know.

Chapter Nine
UNDER THE STARS

Splash of mallard on Wildwood pool
Deep in the woods where summer's cool;
Whirr of a nightjar as he spins,
Twang of a linnet in the whins.

WHAT a deal man misses out of life by lying a-bed! Only homeless men, having the clean earth as a couch, know the beauty of the night, and its inner breathing life. And the world is so changed under the stars and moon that it seems a different place; beautiful, nevertheless, as the daylit world, where the eye can take in the distances at a single glance. There is a freshness and a coldness that is absent in the daytime, and the air seems more pure and clean. And in the woods it is lovely, a ghostly loveliness both rare and splendid. Man shuns the woods at night, and they are empty for the wild folk for hunting and loving, for work and play. Man being a day animal mistrusts the night and its darkness, and has done so from the dawn of his history; and only a very few know the beauties and wizardry of silent trees, standing with their lacing traceries tangled across a dust of stars.

Bellamy Bill, the Woodhall poacher, knew the night and its mysteries, for like Rufus he hunted in the dark hours. And like Rufus, too, though in a much meaner degree, he knew the gateways and the runways of the wild people of the woods. He had seen old Mr. Brocky trotting like a bear down the moonlit rides of a June Coldhangar, he had netted the partridges on the wide rolling fields by Faxton, and many a fine hare had his lurcher pinned by the gateways of Marrow Down. Sometimes, when he found himself in the dock of a police court (this was of frequent occurrence) with the sun streaming in through the windows and the flies buzzing on the ceiling, he would think of the shadow-banded rides of Summermoon, lying ghostly in the moonshine. In Summermoon the old folk said there was a church, and a graveyard, too, now long overgrown with briars and brambles, which few men had ever found. And they said (the old folk) that on wild windy nights, when the trees were talking in the way trees will, the tolling of a bell could be heard, summoning congregations, now long dust, to prayer. Bellamy Bill had found the church and graveyard, and had caught many a rabbit in a snare set by the side of a tombstone, a favourite run for the woodland cottontails. Though he had been abroad in the dark hours for many years he had never seen a spirit, nor heard the wailing of some poor frightened ghost.

To-night he was setting his long net beneath the gate of Marrow Close, for this was a fine field for hares. He worked in the half-shadow of the hedge, lurcher at his heel. The net being set, he motioned his dog into the field with his hand and it slipped away with no more sound than Rufus himself, for he knew his job. This was to circle the big field and start the hares. A hare so disturbed will make for the nearest gateway, and if a net is set he is caught, and the poacher's stick silences swiftly the human screams of terror. The lurcher vanished and Bill was left alone in the hedge bottom, listening to the night wind whispering through the trees. So marvellously still was the sleeping world, the faint whispering seemed loud in his ears, and he could hear the owls in Shortwood, over a mile away. A sheep coughed in a human way over the hedge behind him, where the blackberries rioted in the jungle of the autumn hedge.

He crouched, watching the dim light under the gateway, and his ears strained to catch the slightest sound out in the field. Then a train, puffing northward on the Great Central line, came faintly to him, and the tolling of three o'clock from Wold tower, three lonely notes in the empty silences. Up in the ragged hedge where the leaves were already thinning a blackbird sat, puffed out in a black ball, his head under wing, waiting for the cocks to call up the laggard dawn. All down that hedge sat many birds, likewise asleep though some were wakeful; finches, sparrows, thrushes and magpies, all sleeping, lulled by the whisper of the wind in the dying leaves.

Rufus, hunting across from Old Poors Gorse, with Coldhangar as his ultimate objective, suddenly winded the ranging cur as it glided among the ant-hills. He stopped with upraised paw, trying the air, and then, getting a stronger whiff, he made for the dim gateway at the far end of the field. The lurcher got his scent and ran swiftly, without sound because he had been trained to be silent. Rufus, heard and smelt his swift approach and quickened pace, his brush well off the ground. He went straight for the gate, not to pass beneath it, but through the gap beween the post and the hedge. Bellamy Bill had laid his net well, with due care as to this gap, because hares used the same runaway, and Rufus, travelling with speed, went straight into the net. . . .

A black shadow appeared by the gatepost and the net was agitated and jerked as the fox went in, hopelessly tangled and rolling in a biting ball, all teeth and claws. The heavy ash plant came swiftly with a sullen thick thud on the struggling animal, and it lay still.

Bill, with quivering fingers, undid the net and drew out Rufus by the tail, swearing silent oaths. He laid down the stick and kicked the body on to the side of the road. Then he struck a match and held its quivering light over the still form. Rufus had fallen limply into the hollow of the ditch and the eyes showed no gleam of light. The teeth were slightly bared in a sardonic grin, and in the light of the dying flicker Bellamy Bill saw a flea running over the nose. Swearing softly he gathered up the net and gave a low whistle to his lurcher, which came panting up to the gate on the far side. He would take the fox home with him and skin it, it might fetch a shilling or two in the market town, and it was a fine skin. The lurcher, panting desperately, came through the gap by the gateway, and Bill caught him by the collar, then he picked up his sack and undid the mouth. . . .

When he turned round towards the ditch it was empty. A second ago there had been a dead fox, limply lying where he had been kicked, now there was nothing but a large black slug gleaming in the light of his match. . . .

Rufus had gone, and only the night wind sighed softly in the dying leaves. The blackbird woke up and bustled away with a mad fluttering, and the lurcher dog was chasing into the darkness on the trail of Rufus, unheeding the furious low whistles of Bellamy Bill. . . .

It was lucky for Rufus the blow had been softened by the net, but for many days he felt the ache across his loins, and he came to associate with the man smell an even greater fear and dread than he had before. As for the gateway of Marrow Close, he never passed that way again. . . .

The cubhunters came to Coldhangar a week later, and three of his children perished. The vixen took the remaining cub away to Hieaway, but it would not be tied to her any longer and went its own way, being the second of Rufus's sons to survive the Great Fear. . . . Soon after this Rufus forsook the woods and began to kennel in the hollow of a mighty gnarled oak tree in Lamport Park. This tree was centuries old, and six men could stand inside it, so great was its girth. A pair of Little Owls, which lived in the top storey, were forced to remove elsewhere, and Rufus took sole possession. And no one disturbed him in this snug retreat but the grazing cows who sometimes came to rub their hides against the rugged skin. Woodpeckers and nuthatches sometimes awoke him from his slumbers, pecking loudly and rapping on the rotten wood, and occasionally inquisitive tits would come and scold in the opening above him. But as a rule he slept undisturbed until the light began to dim in the mouth of the hollow and the first stars winked wanly in the darkening sky. Then he would slip out of the aperture and run gracefully down a bending branch, from which he could jump lightly to the ground.

One Sunday, however, towards the end of October, some inquisitive boys came climbing up the tree, and Rufus gave them the fright of their lives when he suddenly emerged just above their heads and ran along the branch. After this, he went away to Hieaway and kennelled there until the first frosts. . . .

On the last night of October Rufus was hunting from Hieaway up the course of the brook towards Draughton. There were a lot of rabbits in the bramble thickets that grew along the stream, and also many young moor-hens, who had not yet reached years of discretion. It was a wild night, and the talk of the stream was drowned by the noise of the wind. Against the dim cloud-scudded sky showers of cold rain came in gusts, rattling the dying leaves and sending them flying into the eddying brook (already high with recent rains). He caught nothing in the bramble thickets and so went along the railway hedge for about half a mile, towards the distant signal and the Draughton crossing.

About fifty yards from the house Rufus decided to cross the line, and seeing a convenient rabbit run through the hedge, he made to slip through. With his usual ease of progress he threaded the runway swiftly and was nearly through when something seized him by the left foreleg. It felt like a cutting ring of molten wire, and the terrified fox rolled and kicked with terror. But Mr. Smollett of the crossing cottage always used strong brass wire for his rabbit snares, and his pegs were long and firmly driven.

For a little while Rufus lay panting on his side, held by this burning devilment of hated Man. He could scent Man smell now, too, on the grass down the bank. From time to time, at intervals of five minutes or so, Rufus gnawed and struggled to free himself, but his efforts were of no avail. Soon a swelling rumble proclaimed an oncoming train, and it passed with a storm of noise and fire along the bank just above him. Even the ground shook at the passing of the tons of steel, and Rufus lay trembling with terror.

The stormy night calmed. So quickly, indeed, had the wind dropped he could now hear the talk of the stream, racing and swirling between the red-brown sandbanks. Overhead the stars peered mistily, and save for sudden fierce gusts of wind that passed through the top of a stunted oak tree by the brook, all became more peaceful. Rufus worked grimly in the shadow of the bank, gnawing the stout cord that held the wire to the peg. Soon he could hear the cocks calling, though dawn was yet some hours away. A rat, running along the cinder path by the line, passed close to him and Rufus smelt it, pausing for an instant and trying the air.

At last, with a jerk, Rufus was free of the peg; but the cutting band of wire had bitten savagely into his left paw, and still held him in a vice-like grip. So tight was the noose, it partially, if not wholly, stopped the circulation, and his foot felt dead and useless. He limped back down the stream, the useless limb numb and swinging, and so he made his way back to the earth in Hieaway under the friendly firs that had seen his birth. In the dark branches the wind sang unceasingly, now with increasing rush, now with gentle murmur like a summer sea. Dawn was greying in the east, and the cocks at Jackman's farm were saluting the valley. Other cocks, too, far away in distant farms answered, and so this message was wirelessed across the county, from farm to farm, from village to village, a wave of merry crowing. It was like the bird song in spring, when the world was turning, and the light of the sun crept up over the dark globe like a tide. For that tide of light is accompanied in springtime by a tide of lovely music, breaking like an advancing tidal bore right across England. But now the woodland birds were silent, tossing asleep and mute in the tree tops, and only the cocks proclaimed themselves the heralds of another day.

Down in the earth, Rufus licked his paw unceasingly and with care, but his sharp ivories could not reach the cruel circle of fire that had bitten so deeply into the draggled black velvet of his foot.

Outside the earth, day had come, and the carrolling of some lusty ploughboy as he clopped with his slow team to work, came faintly on the chill grey morning. Down below, Rufus heard not, only this agony of his poor maimed leg. . . . All that day he worried with his paw, sleeping only fitfully and awaking in starts. In the afternoon, a grey squirrel came and played about round the base of the pine, but Rufus was unheeding. Then, as the dusk fell, the birds came in from the autumn fields to sleep, and a cold rain began to fall. He did not emerge from the earth at dusk, as was his wont, but lay in the warm earth, still working at his paw.

At about nine o'clock, when his belly began to cry for food and urged him to go a-hunting, he rose from his hollow in the sand and pricked his ears. Painfully he dragged himself towards the mouth of the earth, and there he stood for a moment, listening to the patter of the night rain and sniffing the lovely freshness of the wet dark trees. Suddenly he heard something coming up the wood, and a hated whiff sent him, turntail, back into the earth. It was the man smell. . . .

Jim Corfield, the hunt earth-stopper, was coming through the bushes, a little terrier at his heel. He came up to the earth and knelt down, looking inside, and Rufus, below, smelt the man smell and the hairs rose along his back. Not far away from the base of the pine were two billets of wood, fallen fir branches that had once tossed to the winter winds. Jim took these, and wedged them firmly into the mouth of the earth, kicking them home with his big hobnailed boot. Then he went on down the wood, past the box bushes, where there was another enlarged rabbit burrow.

When all was quiet, Rufus went slowly towards the earth's mouth, but it smelt of man and he returned to his couch. But the hunger was on him, and soon, becoming bolder, he went up to the mouth of the earth and found no accustomed opening of dim light, only two tiny cracks through which the sweet air gushed. Puzzled and afraid he returned and lay there miserably licking his paw. . . . The slow hours passed, each hour, each minute, a misery. Then, in the following afternoon, he trembled to hear the Great Fear coming through the trees of Hieaway. The ground telegraphed to him the tattoo of hooves, and in the stifling darkness of the earth he heard the crying of hounds. Footsteps, both of man and beast, rang on the dome of baked dry earth and then went on. Hound noses wuffled at the cracks of the blocked earth, and went away, and all the time Rufus lay, his head on his paws, and his back legs shivering ever so slightly. . . .

Hounds had been running Rufus's vixen (they had found her in Coldhangar). She had come to Hieaway and tried the earths there. Baffled she had gone on to Blueberry Bushes, and there went to ground. They did not dig her out, as it was late, and so she was left in peace. . . .

Just at dusk, steps once more on the bank, and the billets of wood were drawn out. Rufus, down in the earth, felt the sudden rush of pure air surge into the heated chamber, and it was like the opening of a door. Ravening and limping he emerged, when the coast was clear, and went over the fields, painfully, for Cold-hangar. But there the taint of hounds made him turn aside, sick and ill, for the valley. His lameness handicapped him dreadfully, and he was lucky to find a dead rabbit, half eaten by a stoat, lying in the hedge by the crossing spinney. He kennelled that night, not in Hieaway but in the crossing spinney, curling up under a thorn thicket, still licking his tortured paw.

Chapter Ten
IN THE BYRE

Dying rumble of midnight mail,
Song of a ploughman warmed with ale,
Talk of streams in the quiet hours,
Mutter of thunder, drumming showers.

AFTER a week of agony, Rufus, by dint of perseverance, at last worked one of his teeth under the ring of wire. A short jerk, and the noose widened, but he nearly pulled the noose tight again by pulling the wrong length of wire. However, at last he rid himself of the wicked ring of flaming pain, and something made him bury the wire. He took it outside the earth and interred it some distance away in the sandy soil of Hieaway, under the box bushes.

It was most fortunate for Rufus that he had rid himself of the snare or the useless paw would have gangrened and rotted off. Even if it had not poisoned his whole system, it would have so crippled him that the hounds would have soon caught him. For days the paw remained swollen and inflamed and it was some time before he got the feeling back, and could walk the woods with his old effortless stride.

Winter was once again in the land, and by the end of the month (November) most of the leaves were off the trees. In the tall thorn hedges along the Faxton fields the redwings and fieldfares roosted, high up in the topmost straggling branches. These "bullfinches" were a favourite roosting-place for winter visitors, and many magpies, too, always retired to the shelter of the thorny tangles during the winter months.

To the frozen marsh at the head of Lamport pools the little

jack snipe came, questing the rimy bog for food. Rufus, day-hunting, sometimes caught them, winding them as they slept in the reed beds, and many a pheasant he found there, that had foolishly strayed from the park on top of the hill. Very occasionally he caught a sleeping mallard in these same reeds, but the traffic on the adjoining main road scared them away, and, with every autumn, they became more scarce. Another little bird he sometimes scented, but never succeeded in capturing, was the water-rail, shy little red-nosed fellow, that slunk like a mouse through the reeds.

Rufus was now a full-grown fox, of three feet ten and a half inches. His pad had healed, and he was in good condition. Like a wise beast, he hunted his wild haunts cleverly, and with skill; only when the weather was hard did he raid a hen-roost or a yard. One night, when snow was on the ground, he killed seven of Mr. Jackman's chickens, and he even fetched a sucking-pig out of a farrow at the Hawking Tower farm. The squealing of the pig roused the whole farmstead, but he got away, despite the dangerous fury of the distracted sow and the belching muzzle-loader of the farmer.

The long winter nights were good for hunting and he travelled many miles in search of food. But when the stars paled and cattle got up one by one from their well-pressed hollows in the grass, Rufus would turn his nose for Hieaway and its dark comb of firs making low music the hours through. This earth was drier than Coldhangar, and he liked the firs, and the smell of them, and despite the episode of the earth-stopper, he liked this kennel best of all. His vixen hunted with him some nights, but as a rule he led a solitary life and the urge of spring was not yet upon him. So the twain went their own ways and were content.

In the first week of December he changed his kennel for a time, and went back to Badby, a long march away to the south, and he found the great woods to be good and full of game. Pheasants were abundant, and he sometimes managed to get them as they went to roost. And the acres of leafless oaks and puddle-lined rides were to his liking; few folk came there and he was not disturbed. Towards the middle of the month he had an experience that, at the time, gave him a bad scare.

One afternoon he heard shots in the distance, and the barking of a dog. The sounds roused him, and he sat for a while listening, turning this way and that, trying the air. Becoming more uneasy, he slunk away down the side of a green ride, but was brought to a standstill by the sound of more shots directly in front of him. It was a humid grey afternoon, with little breeze moving the tree tops, but scent carried well and he could smell man and dog not far distant. Soon, two terrified pheasants came running past him down the ride, and a minute later another flew across from a belt of fir. More shots . . . a man shouting orders to a dog, and mysterious tapping sounds. Very soon the woods were alive with pheasants and rabbits, creeping past him; all seemed fascinated by the tap-tapping of the beaters' sticks, and Rufus was interested too. The taps drew closer as the line of beaters advanced, and Rufus went with the other fugitives, towards the south side of the woods. Then the pheasants, finding shelter no longer, began to break cover. Some doubled down the leaf-strewn ditches, others took brave wing to cross the valley.

The dry sound of shots crashed out, some all together, others scattered and ringing, and there drifted to Rufus the keen scent of powder. Some of the pheasants were arrested in their steady flight, others went on. A few dropped slanting, and ran like stags back to the cover of the woods, with retrievers hard on their tails. Rufus feared to face the open, so quickened pace along the deep ditch until he left the sounds behind. He realised perhaps that he was not what blood-thirsting man was seeking, so he lay up under a holly thicket and listened to the distant shots. Soon evening came, and all the woods fell silent. Only a scared deer met him face to face, round the corner of a ride. In the thickets he found many wounded pheasants; some were dead, others were alive. These he chased, as they darted under the bushes, "cocking" in terror.

More often he had the scented tree aisles to himself, and his companions were the woodpeckers and woodland birds, the rabbits, and an occasional hare. The staring jay of gaudy wing was his greatest enemy. No matter how thick the underbrush might be, he managed to spy Rufus, and would not leave him until he had every tit and blackbird in the neighbourhood shouting at his heels.

And then what peace in the winter nights, with all the spying jays tucked up asleep, and all the woodland sneaks abed. It was good then, in Badby Woods, with the moonlight lying whitely on the long rides, and the stars pricking overhead. How sweet the woods smelt in those long, long, winter nights! No sound either, but the hoot of an owl, or the early bark of a hunting fox.

These woods were so deserted that Rufus would frequently hunt during the hours of daylight, and for weeks on end he would never see a man. Down one of the rides near the keeper's cottage was a gibbet, and here hung a pitiful array of dried corpses—owls, jays, stoats, weasels, magpies and grey squirrels—and many a night Rufus would come sniffing round the grisly erection and see the wind swinging the pathetic bundles of fur and feather that once were living atoms of warm-blooded life.

In the tall ash trees that grew in the hedge below Hieaway Wood the starlings were clotted on the topmost twigs so that the trees seemed to bear some strange fruit, and the sound of their crashing choirs a great singing wind. Well over a thousand tongues were singing all together, and it seemed like a rush of souls hastening through space. Then, as if at a given signal, all song ceased, and silence fell like a shutting door. Only a distant carrion crow cawed hoarsely in the far distance. Then one starling sang, shyly and small, as though self-conscious of the silence. But in a moment another began, and soon all the mighty voice-rush was in full blast again. Then again the sudden hush . . . and all the thousands of birds began to drop down into the winter sward below, first in scattered groups, then in streams, until the ash trees were bare of birds.

The starlings waddled busily in a compact black carpet, a mass of burnished moving bodies on the drab surface of the meadow. Suddenly, with a whirr, the whole flock lifted, now dense and speckled against the grey sky, now a heavy mass of moving spots. A sparrow hawk had swept out from the firs, and with a lightning swoop was among the darting birds. One starling, squawking violently, darted and twisted as the hawk stooped at it. Then a surprising thing happened; with a lightning stroke the hawk struck downwards with his sharp talons, and the starling's body fell earthwards, headless and with still faint-moving wings. Two feet away the head fell, clean severed from its body. The hawk sailed away round the corner of the hill, his baleful eye scanning the hedgerow ditches. Out in the field the gentle breeze moved the feathers on the headless body as though in pitiful caress.

Rufus, coming up the ditch, had seen the body fall, and he went over to investigate, sniffing it gingerly, and turning away disgusted, for few creatures will eat a starling. So there it lay, with its lovely starred gloss shining to the light as an example of the cruel waste of nature.

Rufus was hungry. His hunting the night before had been unsuccessful and his belly rumbled for food. So he went on down to the brook and across to Coldhangar, sending a flock of sheep by the side of the stream running and bunching, for they thought he was a red dog. Jackman, coming across from Hazelbeech in his milk-float, saw the sheep at gaze and stopped the cart. He caught a glimpse of a red slinking form under the far hedge, and he thought of his raided hen-house with its scattered mangled corpses, and swore softly. His mind travelled back to the farm, to the shelf in the cow house, where he kept a tin, and he vowed to lay Rufus by the heels ere the winter was out. Rufus, all unheeding of this small tea-cupful of grey matter that was reasoning to bring about his downfall, continued up the crab-strewn ditch, his eyes slits in the grey afternoon light as he set his mask for Coldhangar.

He had returned from the fastnesses of Summermoon and Badby, for the love of his old haunts was strong upon him and he yearned for his vixen. But he searched the bare woods and thickets without finding her, and he quested over the old haunts where they used to hunt together, but he never saw her again. The clicketing season was beginning to heat the blood in his veins and he was thinking of another mate. It was now early February and every ditch was full of water to its brim. The brook, so short a time ago dead low, was now running breast-high between its banks, clotting the dead flotsam of winter on the rusty strands of wire stretched across the brook to keep the sheep from straying when the water was at summer level.

Rufus had been lucky to have escaped the Great Fear for so long, and maybe this gave him a sense of false security. However that may be, he took to kennelling, not below ground, but in the reeds of Lamport ponds. A fox likes a dry bed and a warm one, and one might have thought the reeds would have been too damp for him in the marsh, but this was not so. In places they grew so thick, and had done so for years, that they had formed a thick platform whereon he could lie over a foot above the damp ground, and here, screened by thick willow thickets and high spreading reeds, he was secure.

One Monday, in the first week of February, there came the Great Fear, and it found Rufus off his guard. It may be, as I say, that he had grown careless, for an unhunted fox deteriorates in fitness and cunning if left to himself. He had gone to the reeds after killing a chicken at the crossing gate-keeper's pen, and had dined well, which made him sleep soundly. The faint wind, rustling the reeds, lulled him, and he lay curled round like a tired dog, safe from prying eyes. Not even the sneaking jay could see him, so he slept like the dead. A little wren hunting the dead reed jungles hopped past, but she did not notice him, so still he lay; only a very faint heaving moved his red sides as he breathed as gently as a sleeping babe. A rabbit came hopping down a damp trodden run and paused with ears in a V. Its eyes were dilated and the nose worked up and down as it caught the reek of fox. Then it turned back and disappeared. Rufus slept on, full fed and warm. At times his hind legs moved in little jerks as he happily pounced on his game in the woods of dreamland, for a fox dreams like a dog. His heart pumped slowly in his sleeping body, and so sound and deep was he drowned in sleep, that the sentries of his life dozed at their posts though the heavy penalty was death.

Crossing-keeper Herbert Smith had lost many a chicken during the past fortnight and Jackman had also seen the fox about his fields. So maybe a note or a passing word to the Hunt had set matters moving, and already, through the soft winter morning, the hounds were jogging to the Meet at Houghton, the little village that looked over the flashing valley floods. It was not a very big meet, for the Monday country is not a fashionable district, and not more than sixty riders at the most were gathered under the tall elms on the green. . . .

In the morning hounds tried the park and Scaldwell spinney, and drew a blank in both. Then they came pouring down the pretty village street of Lamport and went slowly down the fold of the green valley to Lamport ponds. The field was gathered on the hill top, and some in the road, as the Huntsman took his heart's delight down to the marsh, quietly and without fuss. . . .

A moment or two, as hounds and pink vanished behind the trees and the waving sterns went feathering through the dead docks of the upper marsh. Then, to the watching field on the hill, there came a fierce burst of sudden music, halloing, and the horn. In a moment the little valley was full of sound and the black and pink of the field began to wheel and move, uncertain yet which way the fox had gone. . . .

The first thing that Rufus knew was a big hound pushing

through the reeds not a foot away. Rufus was on his lithe feet in an instant, every nerve alive with sudden fear, for, as we know, the sentries had slept and he was betrayed. The hound saw him and winded him at the same time and lunged forward, crying out. Rufus went straight over the embankment of the middle pool and, seeing the whipper-in sitting his horse on the slope of the field below the road, turned swiftly as a stoat under the rails of the lower pool, emerging in a field below the last willow thickets and making for the railway.

His mind was working with the lightning speed of a seasoned fox, and he knew where he was to go. Coldhangar first . . . and then he would see. The hounds were only a field away, screaming to a breast-high scent with their heads well up, and there was not a moment to lose. The whole hillside down to the pools was alive with galloping horsemen, and many were pouring through the gate by Tyrell's house on the station hill. Two platelayers dropped their spades and ran when they heard the hounds, and they saw Rufus cross the metals and turn up the line for fifty yards before going through the hedge on the other side. He went over the stream, not going through, but springing like a deer from bank to bank, where it swept round a sharp bend by a leaning ash. A green woodpecker swooped away, calling, but Rufus went unheeding up to Hopping Hill. Through the gorse bushes, over the road, and down to the valley and Maidwell Dales.

Cars, travelling along the road, stopped to watch the hunt, but they had not seen Rufus slip like a weasel across the road. Now the field was jumping the brook by the railway, some were thundering up the turf margin of the road and pouring through the gate at the foot of Hopping Hill. Rufus had three fields in hand, but he was not running well because of his orgy of the night before, and several times he was viewed by the huntsman. He passed Maidwell Dales and went straight to Coldhangar, and found, perhaps well for him that day, that the earth was stopped. Jim Corfield had done his work well and thoroughly. Another

Jogging to the meet at Houghton

earth under the ash poles was stopped too, so Rufus turned downhill for Blueberry Bushes. He was not going well, and hounds were hard on his heels. Moreover, he had not the advantage of a dying day, and some instinct told him he was running for his life once more. In his brain was stored the memory of the run from Scaldwell Wood, a hanging tongue and muddied brush. But with the exercise, the effects of his heavy meal began to wear off—he even stopped by the side of a fence and left his card. After that he felt better, and travelled with greater ease.

He set his mask straight down the hill and over the red plough, its fruity slabs, like seasoned Christmas pudding, lying in cheesy furrows that reflected the light and which, in places, was bluesmooth from the plough's keen blade. But even the hounds scarce checked at the cold ground to-day, but came screaming after, thirsting for his skin. Down into the valley then, and up the other side, and here he began to feel the slope. Blueberry Bushes were hidden by the slow rise of the dun-coloured grass, and a mare went a-gallop when she heard the music in the vale.

He threw himself into the thick underwood, and tried the earth under the bushes, but that, too, was blocked, so, never stopping, he went on through the underbrush, and out the other side. At that moment the hounds flung themselves into the wood, scrambling and tearing their way through the dense whitethorn thickets. A huntsman went thudding to the wood below, but he was not in time to see Rufus leave, muddied now and with hanging tongue. There was a check here for the hounds, because other foxes were in the wood, but some terrified sheep betrayed the passage of the hunted fox, and the Huntsman saw enough to get hounds back on the scent. They came streaming up from the purple wooded vale, and Rufus knew they were on him still. And they were gaining now as stealthily and as steadily as a stoat gains on a hunted rabbit. . . .

Sitting in his upturned barrow by the side of the Hazelbeech road the old roadmender was having a satisfying pipe of shag. For some time he had been watching a little robin that was hopping about his feet, picking up his luncheon crumbs. It hopped along in the sandy flints and sodden leaves, cocking an eye at the old man in the barrow. Then, finding no more crumbs, it flew up into the hedge, and, perching on a spray of red berries that matched its waistcoat, trilled a sad little song.

The old man dozed, the pipe slipping sideways in his mouth. For fifty years he had worked on the roads, grubbing like an old badger in ditch and drain; skilful, too, at laying a hedge. When he won the hedge-laying competition twelve years ago it was the most wonderful day of his life, that, and when he married his wife—now gone out of the world. . . .

He awoke suddenly, and pulled out his big turnip watch. "Coo, he musta dropped right off, this wouldn't do, be Gor." . . . At that moment Rufus, a terrible sight, staggered across the narrow lane, not twenty feet away from the roadmender. The old man was so startled at this sudden apparition that the barrow upset and tipped him out on to the grass verge among his turf peelings. When he got painfully up, with many grunts, to his feet, the road lay empty, and the robin had flitted away.

Soon came the cry of the hounds from the direction of Talli Ho! and the narrow road resounded with the cloppings of horses' hooves. The old man stood waving his hat to all and sundry, and then, on bow legs, went staggering uncertainly down the road. Soon the hounds trickled through the hedge like a flood of white yellow-lipped water. With loose strides they crossed the road in twos and threes, and plunged into the little belt of trees opposite.

Down across the park went Rufus, every yard becoming more of an effort. When he had seen the old roadmender he had straightened his back and lifted his brush, and the extra spurt had used him ill. Mercifully, it sometimes happens that a beaten fox does not give off so powerful a scent, and this is especially so after some extra fright or exertion. Certain it was that hounds were hunting more slowly, and though they were only a matter of a few fields behind, Rufus, for a time, held his ground. His last hope, Hieaway, stood dark-crested on its hill over the railway two miles away, on the other side of the valley. He ran through some sheep below the wooded park, and, nearly spent, he reached the railway line. Only another mile now, over the brook, up the little hill, and there was sanctuary and the low hushing of the gentle pines.

Hounds checked at the sheep, but it was obvious where Rufus was making for, and a quick cast brought hounds on to the line. Down from the wooded ridge came the field, turf flying and with drumming hooves. Over the double oxer* at the bottom, Pamela, on Wendy, sailed like a bird, though many a man and woman turned aside for the half-open gate. There was plenty of light yet, and Rufus, unless a miracle happened, was nearly done.

He struggled through the stream and the cold water refreshed him. Then he turned to face the climb to the firs. Those last few yards were agony. With brush right low and arched back, his feet were of lead, and always the cruel grass was before his eyes. Now he could see the dark crest of firs, and with a final effort he entered the wood with the first hound not more than half a field behind. . . .

He went up the steep mound to the earth under the pines. It was blocked. . . .

Jackman, digging a fence hole just below the farm, had heard the cry of the hounds. He put down the long narrow tool and straightened his back, gazing towards the crest of Hieaway. He could see horsemen cantering over the valley floor two miles away, and the pink coats of the huntsmen bobbing along by the side of the line. The hounds he could not see, for they were already up the hill and entering the wood.

*A large fence.

A flock of pigeons left the firs and circled away, and two carrions went flagging out from the lower end, cawing hoarsely, and wheeling. Then he saw the pink coats streaming up to the wood, and black coats mingled. From the heights of Hazelbeech a single rider in black was cantering down, far behind all others. . . . On the Hazelbeech road the old roadman was the recounting his experience to a fellow rustic.

"Cor! I was sittin' in me barrer, when the blurry old fox went right across the road, near knocked me over, 'er did! Looked a game 'un though, bless ye." . . .

All at once Jackman saw a red, draggled slip of a fox coming along the high headland from Hieaway. It was making directly for the farm and Jackman began to run up the hill. It was a spent fox, and was moving slowly; as Jackman ran, he could see the hounds just coming over the ridge with two men in pink cantering on the slope of the field below. With them, but thirty yards behind, rode several of the field and a girl riding sidesaddle. When Jackman came panting up the slope, red of face, and gasping as if he had run a mile, he saw Rufus slip under the muddy gate of the farmyard and go straight into the cow byre at the end of the farm.

"They'll have him, be God!" he swore, still running up the hill. He reached the byre before the first hounds had topped the rise, and entered gingerly, scanning the trampled smelly straw in the corners. Leading out of the byre was a little tumbledown stable where the grey mare was housed, and at one end of this was a manger half full of hay. Standing in one corner was a bundle of planks and poles laid up against the wall, and above this the roof sloped down to the white, stained, plaster.

The fox did not seem to be in the byre, so Jackman went into the stable, scanning the poles in the corner and running his eye along the top of the wall. . . .

With a mighty effort Rufus had gained the byre, and gone straight into the stable. He had climbed the stack of wood and now lay stretched out like a hiding moor-hen, right under the sloping eaves, among the cobwebs. About three feet from his nose was the dried cup of a swallow's nest, with the blue scurf of the babies still in the bottom among the draggled hen feathers. Droppings were still caked on the plaster ledge below. Those swallows were now far, far away, in a land of sand and sun, where white egrets stalked the rice fields by the Nile. . . . His flanks were heaving and his teeth were unclenched, but his eyes and ears were all alive. He heard Jackman come into the byre, and then come below him, treading on the straw and breathing heavily from his run, but he did not move.

He could almost feel the man's eyes scanning the ledge where he lay. . . . A large black spider bustled out of a crack and in again, and in the silence he could hear the sparrows chirp-chirping on the farm buildings outside. . . .

Jackman had seen the tip of Rufus's brush just showing over the edge of the plaster, but he did nothing for a moment. Then with a smile that was meant to be cunning, he went out of the stable into the midden of the yard. The hounds were now all about, sending the white chickens into an ecstasy of terror, and the great gobbler forgot his dignity and ran under the yard gate, head well forward and red wattles swinging. Soon the huntsman came riding up to the gate and Jackman shouted to him. " 'E's in 'ere, seen 'im run into my byre. He's lying top o' the wall!" . . .

The first whipper-in swung himself down from his horse, gathering up the thong of his whip in one hand and handing his horse to another servant. He strode into the byre, calling hounds to him and they gathered round, whimpering for blood. . . .

By now most of the field had come up and were grouped below the farm, their horses steaming from the gallop over the valley, and white lather smeared on velvet skin and top boots. . . .

Rufus, lying on top of the wall, heard the man come through the byre until he stood on the straw below. The sound and smell of the Great Fear was nauseating, but Rufus did not move. He was lying tense and ready for his last spring, and within boiled a fury and a fear. Soon the little stable was full of hounds, and they were making the confined space hideous with their cries. Some were trying to scramble up the poles in the corner, for the reek of fox told them plainly where their prey had gone.

The man let fly with his lash on the white plaster, but the curling thong could not reach the high ledge; only a slab of plaster fell, leaving a sandy stain on the wall. At the slash of the thong Rufus tried to squeeze lower against the rafters, his trembling body pressing against the slates.

Jackman, standing and peering in the doorway, grasped a stout stick. He meant murder, if by some chance the fox got away from the hounds. On the face of things, nothing short of a miracle could save Rufus now. At the end of the ledge stood a rusty golden syrup tin, and in that tin was stored the poison that had killed Rufus's parents. Such is the queer twist of chance.

Unable to move the crouching fox from below, the man called for a box to stand upon, and Jackman soon returned, not with a box, but a short ladder which he used for gathering apples in his orchard. He smiled as he came in, the same cunning smile, for he thought of the tin at the end of the ledge and how it had accounted for many a red robber—how little the Hunt knew!

Meanwhile, the whipper-in had tried to clamber up the planks in the corner, but had only covered his white breeches with dirt and dust, and he slipped back among his clamouring hounds. Several of the Hunt had dismounted now, and were looking in at the open doorway. Rufus still lay motionless, just the tip of his brush showing at the end of the ledge with a cobweb over it. The ladder was brought and the man climbed up three rungs. He could reach the fox now with his thong, and he might have drawn Rufus out. But the floor below was a seething mass of hounds, all watching for the red bolt dropping to their jaws, just as the corpse of a fox is tossed down to the waiting pack in an open kill.

The whipper-in, on a higher level now, could see the top of

Rufus's back over the edge of the white plaster, and he drew back his whip and sent the lash across under the cobwebs. Things happened so quickly that it was difficult to follow. From the end of the shelf bounded the rusty tin, and the tense-strung pack surged upwards like a wave as it fell. But Rufus, his brain working with lightning speed, turned on the narrow ledge, and, at the same moment the tin was sent flying by the lash, leapt backwards over the man's head and down the sloping planks. Only ten hounds saw him, the others were scrambling in the corner where the tin had rolled. He ran in under their legs, by some miracle escaped death by the slashing haste of clicking jaws, scrambled over the back of two hounds and ran between Mr. Jackman's legs. That worthy let fly with his ash plant and Beauty went howling against the wall.

Shouting men, boots, a confused jumble of legs and hooves, and Rufus was out under the gate and went like a red wire along the foot of the yard wall, among the dead stinging nettles. . . .

Within the byre, all was confusion. The man never saw Rufus slip down behind him, for in that second his eyes, like those of his hounds, had been on the bounding tin. But the baffled ten had turned and went streaming out into the yard, calling the others to them. One of the field halloed Rufus away, and in a flash the pack streamed out of the yard, and went singing down the wall.

There was a scramble for mounts, shouts, and the thud of hooves, the squeal of a kicked horse . . . a man's shout. . . .

Mr. Jackman stood by his wife at the entrance to the yard, watching the hunt stream down the slope. "Well, I be . . . the VARMINT!" Jackman was speechless. He went slowly back into the byre and picked up the tin. Luckily the lid was still on and he picked it up and looked at it. "Well, I be. . . ."

The short respite had put new life into Rufus, and he went away down the hill at a great pace, towards the railway, and there, puffing slowly up the line towards Northampton, was a long, rumbling goods train. The driver was leaning out and, together with his fireman, watched the Hunt streaming down the hill. The whipper-in saw the danger and rode like a madman to head his hounds. He won, by a bare forty yards, and with great skill turned the racing pack. His whip cracked like a gun—hounds' lives were at stake.

When the long train of wagons had passed, Rufus had gained five fields, and was making for the crossing spinney. Dusk was falling and the Master gave a reluctant order for home. And so, by the merest thread, the bright life of Rufus was saved. Coincidence, Chance, Pre-ordination, call it what you will, but over the darkling fields went Rufus, slowly now because the sounds of pursuit had died with the rumbling of the train, and he came to Talli Ho! just as the moon was climbing, a great silver plate, above the vaulted trees.

He lay down at the root of an ash, still panting, and deadly weary. High above him rose the moonlit branches, every twig shining in the greenish light, right up and up, until the very topmost twig was reached, a picture of majestic and eerie beauty. . . . Far away a little owl was hooting for its mate, and a lonely peewit called from the moon-drenched wilderness of Penny Plain. He had run a great race and won. . . .

The tip of his right ear was gone, nipped by Ruby in the byre, and from now on he was branded for all men to see.

Chapter Eleven
HALCYON DAYS

Badger's grunt as he digs for bees,
Surf of wind in the forest trees,
Squeak of a bat, and a working mole
Heaving the loam by the elm-tree bole.

THE tide of spring came in again, flooding over the fields and turning them a tender green, and along the brook willow thickets were silver with silky buds. There, by the winding stream, the lambs played under the blue March skies, or bunted and wriggled as they sucked their grave and anxious mothers. Though the nights were still cold, and frost rimed the grass, the early nesters had begun to lay—mistle-thrush, blackbird, song-thrush, and rook. The crossing spinney was once again a twiggy hive of sable life, quarrels were fought, and last year's birds rigorously chased away to form their own colonies in the distant hedgerow elms. The rascally carrions were also thinking about domestic matters in the scattered lonely oaks.

Old Mr. Brocky was no more. The Hunt, running a fox to ground in Coldhangar earlier in the year, had dug the old gentleman out, and he had been killed before the Master could intervene. Every ignorant person will kill a badger, just as they will beat the life out of the harmless and gentle grass snake.

In the warm sun, three grass snakes coiled together among the white anemones, their tongues flickering like fleeting shadows as they writhed about each other. The chiff-chaff had come again, too, and he made Coldhangar bright with his merry music, that told of good things in store for man and beast. Willow warblers again made the thickets murmur with their faery waterfalls. Oh!

happy, hopeful time! "When birds do sing, hey-ding a-ding, a-ding. Sweet lovers love the spring!" And how sweet those lovers are, the little wild people; how coy the hens, how bright and bold the cocks!

On many a high elm branch the lovesick rooks sat pressed together, two and two, and two. The mad hares on Marrow Down, how mad indeed they were, frisking and sparring, jumping and running!

On the green moss of a Coldhangar ride, not far from the coiled snakes, two drab little hedge-sparrow cocks were flirting round a still more dingy hen; and cock blackbirds fought for their ladye loves ... feathers flew. Always the female seems to be the cause of so much pother and disharmony, and as for the robins, they sometimes fought to the death for the lady they loved. Yet soon all these battles would be over, and the families sorted out, all intent on their respective family cares.

The yaffles made the loudest noise perhaps, their laughing cries made the woodlands ring, and there was much boring, and tapping, and weaving, and smoothing. Two big grey mistle-thrushes were the busiest of them all, flying to and fro with gigantic beakfuls of the greenest moss, to the big oak at the top of Coldhangar Wood. The hen would get inside the mossy hollow and tread it with her feet, turning round and round and pushing downwards and outwards with her wings, to form the perfect cup for her not far distant eggs. Did any bird venture near then, "Scrrrrrrrrrrrrrrrrrrrr, be off with you," they would cry, and even the jays were afraid, and fled raggedly into the thickets, using the vilest language. Soon, for the jays, it would be "egg time," and what a harvest they gathered, later on, from field and wood.

Not only were the feathered folk busy a-wooing and nesting. Rabbits were already tending families in the nesting burrows. Just outside Coldhangar, close to the furze, an old doe had dug a burrow for her babies. This she sealed up every time she left it, smoothing down the earth and grass, and so fastening her little pink infants safely in their nursery. It is something of a mystery how baby rabbits breathe, for the entrance to the hole allows of little ventilation, and the breeding earth has no other exit. But alas! for the gentle doe, who denudes her very breast of down to keep her babies warm, the foxes and the badgers often found the nests and dug them out, and Rufus had many a tasty meal in the early spring and summer. . . .

Up in the old earth under the rhododendrons, Rufus had another lusty family of cubs, this time by a Talli Ho! vixen. His first-born son had been killed in the early winter by the hounds, after a straight-necked run from Scaldwell Wood. He had died gamely, as befitted a son of Rufus, in the open beyond Blue Covert, fighting till the last.

His other son of the second year was still alive and had a family of three cubs in Old Poors Gorse. As for Rufus, now at the prime of life, he was the perfect fox. Not perhaps as far as coloration or size, but for gameness and cunning he had no equal in all the Pytchley country from Sulby to Rushden. Jackman did his damnedest with trap and snare, but Rufus was aware of him, and since the episode of the byre he gave the farm a wide berth. The farmer blamed him for taking lambs, but this was untrue. Rufus took dying and dead lambs, but never a lusty youngster, and the pathetic little corpses were far better utilised feeding the young cubs than rotting in some ditch. Rufus only killed for food. Even when he burst out into an orgy of chicken killing, he was killing for food, though he might not be able to eat all he slaughtered. As a general rule he only killed in districts that were away from his earth, and in this way he was a true hunter, whereas the men who came after Rufus with hounds were not true hunters at all, for they did not kill for food, like the fisherman or the gunner. And it was no use saying that they hunted the fox because he was such a pest, for the next moment they were making specially built dens for foxes in the woods, wherein they might breed undisturbed.

The whole population of the Midland foxes could be wiped out in a very short time if serious measures were taken, but in exchange for the pleasure man found in horse-craft and hound-craft when hunting the fox, he had given him continued life and on the face of things this seemed a good bargain. A fox, in a well-supplied district, is seldom hunted more than twice in a season, and if, like Rufus, it can survive several runs, the chances of its being caught become more and more remote. Hunting with hounds is cruel, however, and man knows it to be cruel; the whole of Life is cruel, or, shall we say, unfeeling.

Every hunting-man likes the chase because it involves some risk, and a man who rides straight must possess a good courage. So it is no coward's game. If, as we learn on good authority, a man's life is worth many sparrows, we may take it it is worth many foxes, too, and if we total up the number of fatalities in the hunting-field since the sport first began in England, we may think the fox wins (as he usually does) in the end. . . .

Rufus had brought his family a rabbit for supper, and the cubs were tearing and worrying at the carcase, some even getting right inside with shocking debauchery.

Late thrushes were singing both near and far, and the pigeons had already come down off the high trees into the ash poles and were preparing for sleep. In the wood pool the trees, naked yet and without leaf, were reflected with faithfulness; only a shaking ring from some questing water-hen broke the shining pool set in the dark bushes.

Rufus left his vixen and happy family, and went away by himself to the pool. Animals experience happiness, or more properly a feeling of great content, and to-night Rufus felt at peace with the whole world. Spring was coming, if not already here, though the leaves were yet sticky unfolded buds on the bare branches. And with the summer came content, plenty of game, and no hounds clamouring for his blood. He was thirsty, and after a look round, he went over the bank and down to the margin of sodden leaves.

As he drank the circles went shaking out across the water, and the shadow of a great tawny owl passed over the bright mirror.

To the west, behind the bare poles that swayed ever so slightly to a thin cold breeze, squeaking and rustling, the sun had set in a blaze of yellow and gold. Tiny little cloudlets, pink tinted, were combed out across the sky, and against them the gently swaying poles stood in sharp relief. After drinking, Rufus went to the bole of a holly and rubbed himself like a horse. He stretched, opening wide his mouth and laying back his ears, then stole over the bank again and went on down through the darkling trees. Everywhere the wreckage of the past winter was evident, heaps of dead and dying leaves, rotting down to form the rich, dark mould of the forest floor.

That night, with the moon a week old, hanging like a silver bow in the eastern sky, he hunted across to Talli Ho! and killed a rabbit on the outskirts of the wood just as dawn was breaking over the wooded hills. Life was good, life was sweet, and the whole of the summer was before him. What joys, what adventures would it bring? He puzzled not at the mysterious rebirth of life, and he did not concern himself in great matters that were beyond him. Man, who, because he had a beginning and an end, was ever wrestling with the problem of the chicken and the egg, "which came first," was less at peace than this wild child of the woods, roaming his well-loved lands. Just as children are more intelligent than we believe them to be, so, I think, it is with animals; they feel pain more acutely than we think, and, though within a beast's body, their grave eyes are aware of things we little guess or understand. . . .

Pamela was sitting in a deck-chair on the tennis-lawn, one leg stretched out, with the ankle bandaged and propped up on a chair, watching Pipeete the bat hawking round the scented limes. She had sprained her ankle while playing squash, and for the last fortnight had been crippled. An unread book lay, leaves open, on the close-mown grass. She was watching the slow dimming of the summer dusk making much mystery of the fragrant garden.

In the lily-pool the roach were cruising about, crinkling the bright surface as they caught the little flies, and the lily-buds were tight shut after the heat of the day.

Moths banged about among the hollyhocks in the border, and over the dark shrubberies the first stars were lit, pale points of light that trembled, then hung still. Through the trees she could see the peaceful valley, misted with the soft coming of the June night, and on a far hill a cottage light starred out, a vivid spark that shamed the evening stars. From under the iron railings in the park she saw a dark shape steal, and after a moment's pause, go out across the grass. Behind there followed three smaller spots of shadow, running swiftly after. It was Rufus's vixen, taking her children hunting. She came past the end of the lawn, stopping ever and again, and looking towards the house and lawn and the white figure stretched in the deck chair, disappeared behind the far trees, the cubs still scrambling after her.

Not very long afterwards a hedgehog came out from under the peonies, busily rooting from side to side. It went right across the lawn, past the watching girl, and vanished in the dark shrubberies. . . . What adventure was abroad in the summer dusk!

For a fleeting moment Pamela realised the life of the woodland people, this furtive hunting under the stars. How far away the days of winter seemed, with the music of the hounds and the purple bare woods and ashen fields! Overhead Pipeete still circled with flickering wings, and a rabbit went hopping down the distant terrace, shaking his hind pad like a cat. . . .

On the lawn lay the stubs of cigarettes and several empty chairs; Pamela's friends had departed; gay youngsters, bubbling over with good spirits and youth. Their noisy sports cars had long since roared down the winding drive. Large black slugs were abroad on the tennis lawn, and the hedgehogs went bustling across the white lines that glimmered in the dusk. . . . How few people knew or cared for wild life! This world of little people she now saw going about their business in the scented gloaming of the June night. . . . Those skylarking youngsters never gave them a thought, so taken up were they with their own artificial world where pleasure-seeking became a drug. . . . Heated rooms, cocktail bars, the empty silly flirtations . . . the shallowness of it all.

A sudden yapping in the quiet announced that Peter, the white Highland, had discovered the hedgehog in the herbaceous border, and his baffled shouts called for human aid, so Pamela limped down the long path, past the rambler roses, to the rescue. She found the ball of indignant spines under the delphiniums and drove Peter away. Although she stood watching the hedgehog for a quarter of an hour, it did not unroll, so she went away up the path to the house, a sulky Peter following at her heels. . . .

Five fields away, in the lush dewy grass, the vixen was teaching her babies how to stalk field-mice, and nobody saw them but the white owl, beating the hillside on gliding wings . . . flap, flap, flap . . . glide . . . he passed right over them, and his ghostly form made the cubs run to their mother's side. . . .

And so passed the halcyon days, the pageantry of an English summer in full array, with its happy goldfinches with wings like spokes of gold; the awesome music of the nightingales in Coldhangar, the well-loved mossy rides where no man came.

Sometimes, when the sun shone warm in the clearings of the forest, Rufus lay stretched like a cat before the fire, warming his stomach and stretching his legs. Had it not been for the tin on the end of the byre ledge he would not be here, on the warm bank among the bobbing meadow browns. . . . Sometimes he tried to catch these butterflies, but they were too quick for him, and seemed to see him coming out of their staring painted eyes at the tips of their wings. . . . And then, when the sun slanted down behind the trees and the swifts went scything high, so high, in the upper atmosphere, he would pad away under the whitethorn, following the paths he knew so well. Some of these paths were quite bare in places from the passing of the secret woodland folk. Frequently he met great velvet bumble bees threading their way through the close-crowded stems, and he would back and click his teeth.

Once, near the wood pool, he heard the sounds of a fight. "Tissings," and scufflings. When he peered over the bank he saw a large stoat and a rat circling round one another. Sometimes they stood up on their hind legs and boxed, now they jumped and sprang, but the rat was driven back to the edge of the water. He dare not turn to face his antagonist or the stoat would have been on him in a moment. At last the stoat gave a lightning spring and a squeal rang out as the cruel little teeth met in the rat's neck. Rufus slipped down the bank and was on the stoat before it realised it. It swore and bit, rolling over and showing its sulphur belly, but Rufus seized it by the neck and shook it from side to side, savagely. Even then it was not dead, but tried to scurry, drunkenly, away. Then with a bound Rufus had him again and killed him. He ate the rat, but would not eat the stinking stoat, though he carried it up the slope and rolled on it because the smell was bad. Then he went down to the water and had a drink. . . .

Every ditch and hedgebottom which was bare and damp some months back, was now a jungle of lady's bedstraw and nettle, wherein he found the hapless partridge brooding her nest. Sometimes he found a hen pheasant, but they were rare in Coldhangar. . . .

Then the birds fell silent, and the heated woods seemed waiting for something to happen. Only the robin let fall his tender reminder of the joys of autumn once again. The first trees to burn were the big chestnuts by Lamport ponds, and soon the conflagration spread up the foliage like a torch, until they were all afire with a riot of colour. Wild duck came again to the wood pool in the evenings, and Rufus's family, lusty now, and able to fend for themselves, were all over Coldhangar in the darkling. Rufus sometimes went with them, but as a rule he hunted on his wild lone, as did the vixen. . . .

Down one of the rides in Coldhangar there was a great oak, ivy-clad to three-quarters of its height, and much sought after as a nursery by the woodland birds. The great hairy arms of the ivy-roots were easy to ascend, and one day Rufus, feeling bored, climbed up. A grey squirrel saw the agitated ivy, and came over to a nearby branch, where he scolded at Rufus with bottle-shaped brush. Rufus heard the sound and peered with his cunning slits of eyes through the interstices of the ivy leaves. The wily squirrel kept his distance, for he knew there was danger. But the noise he made brought several blackbirds, always hysterical busy-bodies, and for a while the noise was dreadful.

Rufus lay in a fork of the tree, right amongst the ivy, and let them get wearied and go away. Even the squirrel got tired of the sport, and jumped away over the arching branches. When all was quiet once more Rufus continued his climb, for his sharp nose told him that there was a nice bird smell somewhere close at hand. . . .

He hauled himself up another couple of feet to another fork, and then he had the fright of his life. There was a sudden great clapper of wings and a bustling that nearly made him jump out of the tree. A great blue wood-pigeon went away through the trees, his staring eye more round than ever with fear. When he had got over his fright, Rufus peeped through the fork and found himself looking into a platform of sticks on which sat two upright squabs, a late brood even for a wood-pigeon. They had partially got their feathers, clusters of blue quills from which the feathers were bursting like leaves from a sheath, and they were covered with coarse yellow down, almost like hair. They had seen Rufus and were now raised in the nest, their broad, soft bills slappering with fright, and every now and then they made lunges at the watching fox. He jumped down on the nest in the fork and grabbed one squab. It was very good. He killed the other, too, before it could escape, but it dropped off the flimsy structure and went crashing down through the ivy on the green moss below.

Rufus ate the first squab in the fork, then he went down the trunk and devoured the other. . . . When the mild, grey mother returned to the tree she found her nest all askew, and drops of blood, showing rich, dark red on the spattered sticks, and bits of white down everywhere, blowing in the breeze. She sat pondering for a long while, and then, still not understanding, flew away uncomfortably. . . . The ash-pole pigeons Rufus could not harm, unless one youngster fell off the nest, and this sometimes happened when there was a gale of wind, but he would look up at the black structures longingly to where a black wedge of a tail protruded.

A curious fact about these pigeons was that though their eggs, being white, were so conspicuous, the woodland robbers, jays, magpies and carrion crows, rarely pillaged them.

And so that summer passed.

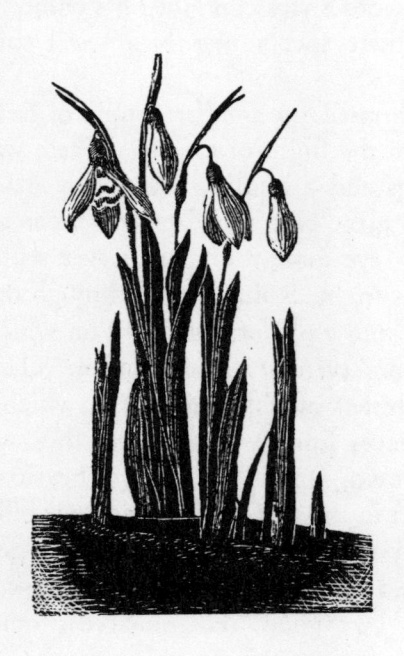

They were covered with coarse yellow down

Chapter Twelve
GIPSY LANE

Scent of the plants in ditch and dell,
A long-dead rabbit (lovely smell!)
Nettles and hemlock, elder bloom,
Perfumed oak woods, seeded broom.

To the east of Blueberry Bushes there is a winding, gated lane that leads, after many deviations and with the happy meanderings of a brook, to join up with the main road a mile and a half away. For the first part of its length it is hedged on either hand with tall ragged bullfinches, red now with the hips and haws and glorious riot of deadly nightshade. Wide turf margins open out as the lane proceeds, until finally the fields are reached. Up this lane one evening towards the end of October, there came a ragged cavalcade of gipsies with a hooded caravan.

First came two women, one old and withered, with a crinkled, dark face, the other a young girl of fifteen or thereabouts, a lovely child whose face was as vivid in its beauty as the trailing festoons of autumn berries glowing in the wreckage of the hedges. Over their arms they carried wicker baskets filled with clothes pegs. The girl's slim, honey-coloured legs were bare, and the tattered skirt scarce reached her knees. Behind, came the caravan, drawn by a well-fed, fat, grey horse, and a middle-aged man sat hunched on the shafts, a scarlet neckerchief round his throat, and a short pipe between his teeth. Under the caravan, between the wheels, ran two dogs, as cunning as their lord and master riding up aloft. Tied to the caravan was a small tilt cart with a swinging bucket underneath, and within the cart, in addition to an extraordinary assortment of articles, lay a bicycle, tied on its side by a stout cord passed under the floor of the cart. Bringing up the rear of this picturesque cavalcade, a small, rough-headed boy followed, a stick in his hand, chewing a twig.

They conversed together as they journeyed, these wild and happy folk, in shrill squealing tones, like the yapping of dingoes. Coming to a place where the lane widened somewhat and a little brook ran under the road through a culvert, they stopped, and the horse was taken out of the shafts. After a knotted rag was tied between his forelegs, he was turned out to graze on the green grass. All was bustle and commotion, though they worked with the air of each having a definite job to do. The cart was unhitched from the back of the caravan, and the bicycle untied and set against one wheel of the tilt. The women went along the ditch, collecting firing, and the man walked slowly down the lane with the dogs, his sharp eyes scanning the ditch for a rabbit run in which to set a snare.

Soon the lurchers went down into the ditch bottom, among the dead leaves and brambles. A little while after there was a faint suppressed yelp and a rabbit, half-grown, tore across the road, both lurchers hard on its heels, and a moment later a squeal, cut short with a suddenness, told of a kill. The gipsy, after a quick, fox-like look up and down the lane, got down into the steep ditch and blackberry bushes, and emerged with a bulge, a warm bulge, under his coat. The two lurchers trotted innocently at his heels as he went back to the encampment. When he turned the corner of the lane he saw the blue smoke of the fire misting through the tawny bushes, and there came to him a lovely reek of burning faggots. The women were busy about the fire already glowing redly in the dusk and flickering on the open door of the caravan.

He walked to the tilt and lifting the corner of a sack, pushed the rabbit's warm body underneath, a needless precaution, for very rarely did anyone come along the lane, and the grass grew where once the stage coaches bowled along to the merry music of the post horn.

As the dusk deepened into the velvet pall of night the fire became more vivid, showing the autumn glory of the trees and bushes, and lighting the interesting faces of these wild people. They differed from the usual country clods one sees in the rural villages, whose faces are as expressionless as cows. It is seldom one sees an uninteresting gipsy face, even in the old people. Soon the fire crackled merrily as they lay about it, and in the dancing light of the ruddy flames, the face of the young gipsy girl seemed of a beauty not of this earth.

Gradually the fire died down, subsiding with rustling clicks, and outside the warm circle the night air struck cold and damp on the gipsies' backs. So with many wranglings and bickerings the family retired within the caravan. As for the lurcher dogs, one went with the family, and the other was tied to the wheel, where it lay nose on paws, eyes fixed on the dying embers of the fire. . . .

Rufus was in mischievous mood, for he was hungry. More rabbit catchers had been at work in the furze of Blueberry and Coldhangar, and the stock was sadly depleted. Moreover, the unreasonable farmers had taken undue precautions with their fowls and poultry, for Rufus was unfortunately beginning to be known to the country people for his daring and cunning. This was an unfortunate state of affairs, because it meant every man's hand was against him, and since the episode of Jackman's farm, he was known by sight to the Hunt and country people. Rufus, the one-eared fox, a criminal of the deepest dye, whom no hound or man could ever catch, or snare. . . .

Rufus came across from Coldhangar in the early dawn. He was on his way to Hieaway, where for the last week or so he had been kennelling. He had had no game, hunting was bad. Therefore, he was in mischievous mood, and so prepared to run risks. Half-way across Penny Plain, where the restless peewits roosted among the ant-hills, his sharp nose caught the smell of fire, and he stopped, deliberating. There were also other smells, of man and dogs and refuse, so he decided to investigate. He slipped through the ragged bullfinch fifty yards above the sleeping encampment, and stopped on the grass verge, trying the air.

He saw the still, rounded hump of the caravan against the hedge, and a few dull red cinders before the door, which threw a faint glow on the spokes of the wheels. Above was the arch of stars, a little pale now because an unearthly greenish tinge suffused the eastern sky, as the light began to filter over the curve of the earth. But what interested him most was a strong smell of rabbit coming from the tilt cart at the back of the caravan, and so, very slowly, he stole forward along the bottom of the hedge, stopping ever and again to listen and sniff. As he drew nearer the scent of fresh-killed rabbit grew stronger, and the smell made him feel very hungry.

Beneath the caravan lay the cur, fast asleep, talking and twitching because subconscious senses told of a strange smell, and the scent became entangled in its dreams. It was that time when all day-hunting animals, man included, sleep most soundly in the open air, and even the cocks were fast a-slumber. The red sparks of the almost dead fire shone like rubies in the darkness, and a faint breeze, coming from beyond the fire to Rufus, sent a little tiny spark into the grass between the wheels of the caravan. Still the cur slept, and in the caravan, the gipsies slept too, snoring like owls. Only the girl lay awake, lying on her back with a moth-eaten fur coat drawn over her slim lovely body, staring through the chink of the half-drawn curtains, at a little wistful star. . . .

Rufus came up to the tilt cart, and stood on his hind legs, resting his forepaws on the shafts, and sniffing the crack between the tail-board and the floor. The scent of rabbit was very strong, and was obviously just under the sacking. He took one more peep at the sleeping cur, then jumped nimbly, with the beautiful grace of a panther, on to the top of the tail-board.

On his way to Hieaway

Within the caravan the gipsy father stirred in his sleep muttering plaintively, and the snores of the other inmates died to a soft breathing. The fox heard the muttering of the man and leapt lightly down to the grass again, ready to vanish into the shadows. But all was still, the cur slept on. After waiting a moment, Rufus again leapt on the cart and poked his nose under the sack. He pulled the rabbit out, but put it down for an instant, listening, for the cur was stirring below; a back eddy of breeze had brought the reek of fox to his sleeping senses. Rufus stood on top of the dusky cart, his one erect ear giving him an even more tense appearance. Then he picked up the rabbit and turned round to run down the shaft of the cart. At that moment, the cur was wide awake and sprang to its feet, eyes dilated and ears cocked. Immediately his awake senses told him all was not well, and he went off into a paroxysm of staccato barks that split the silence like a knife.

Inside the caravan, the other cur awoke and bounded to the door. The man awoke, cursing and muttering, still half-dazed with the drugs of slumber, and pushed his head out. . . .

Rufus, with the rabbit in his jaws, leapt off the top of the cart, and at the same moment, the cur jumped out of the caravan and was hard on his heels. Under the caravan the other dog leapt and strangled at his string, his wild yapping choked in his throat. What excitement then to be sure! The man shouting, the women screaming angrily at this sudden disturbance, and the ragged urchin jumped to the ground and stood looking after the departing cur that was hard on the heels of Rufus. The latter had dropped the rabbit when he found the dog gaining on him, and, badly frightened, dived into the culvert. He ran through the shallow water that was not more than two inches deep at the most, to the far end, and there he found his way barred by an iron grating . . . he was trapped! The cur had followed him in and was a plucky scoundrel. He flew at the fox, who turned about and faced him, and in the confined space they bit and worried savagely. Rufus was a match for the light-built dog, and he drove him back yard by yard towards the mouth of the culvert. Meanwhile, the gipsy urchin and his father came up with the other dog, a thicker-set beast with a dash of terrier in his blood, who was afraid of nothing. The bleeding cur backed out, tail between legs and "ki-wi-ing" plaintively, and the gipsy shouted to the boy to fetch a sack from the tilt cart. . . . A fox's skin might fetch a few shillings. . . .

Telling the terrier to guard the entrance, he ran to the other end of the culvert, stumbling down the bank in the half-darkness of the dawn. He saw the iron grating and realised the fox was unable to get out. Then he felt the grating and found it loose in its socket and he called the boy down the bank to him there. He lifted the grating out and fixed the mouth of the sack in position, laying a stone on the bottom inside edge and holding the top edge against the upper rim of the cement drain.

By now the dawn had greyed sufficiently to reveal the dew-wet hedges and the green-painted van drawn up on the grass, and at the door the women, shading their eyes.

"Goo you to t'other end and send Grip into him, you," shouted the gipsy. So the boy urged the terrier into the drain, while the whippet stood with trembling hind quarters by the mouth of the hole, not daring to face those teeth again. Rufus in the culvert saw the sudden darkening of the dim light at the grating end, and the dark form of the terrier coming towards him down the tunnel, its hairs on end and growling savagely. . . .

For a moment there was a tense silence, the gipsy waiting crouched over the sack, and his strong brown hands clutching the folds. . . . A faint subterranean yapping, sounds of a scuffle, and something shot like a bolt into the sack. Like a flash the gipsy raised it, closing the top, and with the struggling animal inside it, climbed triumphantly up the bank.

"I got the b——. Gie I a big stick." . . . He carried the sack to the top of the bank, and taking the stick from the boy, hit the squirming sack a sickening blow. Within, all movement ceased.

The man, with his white teeth showing in a bestial grin, held the sack upside down, and there dropped out on the dewy grass—the body of the terrier cur with its back broken. . . .

Neither had realised that the terrier had not come out of the culvert, and by now Rufus was speeding across the grey fields to Hieaway, his body smarting with two savage bites on his flank. Once he stopped and glanced back, his sly eyes slits, the one ear cocked like a question mark. From over the ragged rust of the hedge a faint, blue smoke was drifting, and the sound of wrangling and screams were borne to him on the breeze. The gipsies were all talking at once, and the sound was as of a lot of jackals on a kill.

Rufus cocked his leg against a dead thistle and went on down into the dewy valley where the early rooks were getting their breakfast. Mushrooms gleamed in the grass like white stones, and on one of them, nibbling the luscious pink flesh, a huge black slug was sprawled. Rufus sniffed it, took it in his teeth and shook it, throwing it away into the grass.

He went into Hieaway under the gate and slunk up to the box bushes. And there he was lulled to sleep by the rush of the wind in the dark firs, for no one came near the wood all day. He slept till a blackbird awoke him, and he found the sun setting behind the grill of trees, now almost bare in the upper branches that showed so blackly against the tender sky.

WILD VIOLET

Chapter Thirteen
MYSTERY OF PENNY PLAIN

Jugging partridge upon the fallow,
Water dock where the stream runs shallow,
Stack-yard foil and a runner duck,
Steaming hill of Jackman's "muck."

"IF YOU asks me, it's none other than an old badger boar; look at that beast they dug outer Coldhangar last year." Bellamy Bill put his tankard down on the top of the bar and wiped his mouth with the back of his hand.

The keeper, sitting in the corner by the dart board, shook his head. "In all me years a-keeperin' I never knew a badger to take anything bigger un a rabbut, Bill, and 'e'd never tackle a ship, or a lamb, for that matter; 'e ain't quick enough on 'is pins."

"Well, if it ain't a badger, it's that ole fox wi' one ear that diddled the 'ounds up at Jackman's last year, 'e's cunnin' enough, and strong enough, to kill a calf." Bellamy Bill's mind was dwelling on the night up at Marrow Close, though as to his activities there he kept silent.

The keeper shook his head slowly, and spat into the sawdust of the spittoon on the floor. He knew all about Bellamy Bill and had a great contempt for him.

"Whatever it be, it's got to be shot, or there won't be a ship left on the farm." The keeper got to his feet and put his pipe in his pocket. "Mr. Thomson's offered five pun' to the man 'oo shoots it, whether it be fox, badger, or dog, but ef it turned out to be a badger, Bill, or even a fox, I'll gie 'ee free leave to kill every pheasant in my wood, an' I'm thinkin' that's a safe bet; what d'you say, landlord?"

"Well, keeper, I've lived in the country all me life, born and bred as you might say, an' I know enough to say no fox, nor yet a badger, would look at a grown ship. A lamb perhaps they might take, but a full-grown ship, no."

The keeper, after bidding the assembled company good-night, stumped out of the bar. After he had gone a silence fell on the company, as though they were waiting for him to get out of earshot. Then Bellamy Bill, draining his tankard and looking round with an air of superiority, gave a sneering laugh.

"Ah, 'e's little Johnny-know-all, 'e is. I reckon I know more about wild animals than Keeper Thorn; allus layin' down the law. Badgers be powerful beasts, an' they've got a bite wi' 'em that'll take an ox's leg off almost. Why, didn't my Granfer 'ave 'is 'and near bitten off be one that got in 'is net one night up at Coldhangar?"

"Ah, that's wot become o' poachin', Bellamy," laughed the landlord. "Reckon the old gentleman was a bit sobered arter that, weren't 'e? They do say the constable's bin up at Windy Hill for the last wick, but 'e didn't see nothin'," said the landlord, hastily, in case his last remark had touched a tender spot with his patron. "An' Mr. Jackman an' a lot more o' the farmers round 'ave bin awaitin' up wi' guns. But I reckon they don't keep watch proper; there's a nice 'aystack up in the top o' the meadow, an' there's nothin' like a 'aystack for a warm bed, specially arter a pint or two of my double-X ale!"

"Ah, they can watch an' watch," said Bellamy, "but they'll niver get that beast whatever 'e be. Why, they smoke their pipes all the time an' never study the wind. Might as well try an' put salt on 'is tail. There's only one way o' gettin' that baste, whatever 'e be, ef it is a baste," he added darkly. "An' that's by poison. Poison be wunnerful stuff ef you use it proper, an' don't touch the carcase wi' your bare 'ands. Maybe it's a 'untin' dawg that's gone bad, an' that's the worst sorter baste to 'ave anything to do wi', they gets that artful they won't look at poison, an' only 'unt be night. Why, it might be a dog from the other side of the county, for I've known 'em to travel miles to kill, an' get back afore it's light." . . . And so the talk went on in many of the inns and ale-houses in the district, and men knew not where the killer would strike next.

One week, five sheep were found dead in Marrow Down, and a fortnight later Mr. Hardmuth, up at Willow Tree Farm, lost seven, all killed in the night when the moon was young. Many a cold vigil was spent by anxious farmers, peering into the darkness from stack and byre, but they never saw the killer or heard him strike.

As for Bellamy Bill, he was uneasy at this mystery, for his nocturnal poachings had to be conducted with more care. Many times he met shadowy figures coming along lonely roads, guns over shoulders and dogs at heel, and he was forced to go wider afield for his nightly forays. . . .

But there was one farmer whose stock seemed to bear a charmed life, and that was Mr. Jackman. In the five weeks since the killing began he had not lost a single sheep, though the farm across the valley, not far from Coldhangar, lost two sheep from out of a flock close to the farm. . . .

Then, Mr. Johnson of Windy Hill, trotting round his fields one early morning, came on the body of a sheep lying in the ditch with its throat torn out. The other sheep in the field were bunched and nervous as though they had been run during the night, and it was evident the midnight murderer was up to his evil tricks once more. Farmers again folded their sheep close to the farmsteads and set men with guns to guard them, and the local press sat up and took notice. Then the London dailies took it up, and reporters with notebooks were seen in the village streets. There was a photo of Mr. Johnson on the front page of *The Morning Star*, standing with his double-barrelled gun by the corpse of the murdered sheep. . . .

The wide sweep of Penny Plain, studded with its ant-hills, lay vacant to the stars. Through the dead thin bents a wicked little wind played, ruffling the feathers of the roosting peewits, and shaking their handsome crests. Now and again one of the birds shifted and complained petulantly . . . "Pee-weee, pee-weee." The thread of shrill sound reached the ears of the farmer, lying on the windward side of the haystack by the western hedge, and he peered into the darkness, turning his head to catch the slightest sound out in the lonely field.

Not far away the woolly sheep moved about in their pen of hurdles, some cropping the grass (the farmer could hear the sound of tearing), and a muffled bleat now and then as they moved about the fold. But for the most part the night was still, and the usual night sounds—bark of a distant dog, the restless peewits among the ant-hills, and the hoot of an owl—gave but a hint of the stirrings of beasts and birds under the cloak of darkness. Overhead a few filmy clouds hurried, as though on urgent business which must be transacted before the coming of the dawn. The man lay back in the warm hay looking at the little points of remote stars that glistened like jewels in the roof of a mighty cave. Now and again the hay rustled as the wind caught it, or some questing rat scurried like a ferret after a mouse. Mr. Johnson was a sociable soul, and these nightly watches were not to his taste. Better far to be tucked up in bed with his ample, cosy wife, with warm blankets round him, sleeping an untroubled sleep!

This killer by night must be done to death, however, and as he lay there he wondered what manner of creature it was that could pull down a full-grown sheep and tear its throat out. Could it be some wolf, escaped from Whipsnade Zoo? After all, the place was not very far away and he had seen the fierce beasts many times, loping under their dark firs and tearing their meat at feeding time. He remembered one great grey fellow that *would* come behind the keeper, making lithe lunges forward as the man threw the red gobbets of flesh from the bucket. . . . He was not an imaginative man, but to-night he seemed to be imagining all sorts of things. After all, what did man know of the dark hours, or what creatures might be abroad? Somewhere, in this sleeping country-side, roamed the killer, a bestial Jack the Ripper, whom no man had seen.

He moved uneasily in the hay and felt the cold steel of the double-barrel. His finger pushed at the safety catch to make sure the gun was cocked. In the dimness a large rat scurried busily along the base of the rick, and for a second his eyes caught a glimpse of the sinister form. Yes, there was no doubt about it, this business was nerve-racking, even for a man of Mr. Johnson's mentality. He pulled out his watch and held it close to his eyes . . . half-past one. . . . Soon he would give it up and go home; after all, the killer had not been for the last five nights, and it was doubtful if he would show up now; the sheep seemed to be contented in the fold . . . perhaps the beast had gone elsewhere.

The faint breeze whispered in the strands of hay, and the warmth of the stack began to induce a certain drowsiness. A little nap, perhaps, and then, if nothing was heard, he would go home to the farm. . . .

A brown owl came silently over Penny Plain, beat over the huddled forms of the sheep in the fold, and lit on top of one of the pegs in the top of the haystack. It sat there like a gargoyle, turning its huge head from side to side, looking for mice moving down below. It did not see the man curled up in the hay beneath, and after a while it flitted away, soon to be lost in the shadows. As the slow hours passed more clouds drifted up from the south-west, travelling more slowly now, and dimming the stars. It was very cold, with that killing cold that comes before the coming of the life-giving sun.

One by one the sheep lay down, until all were lying with their feet tucked under them. Some chewed sleepily, and others slept, and in the hay the farmer was asleep, too, his head lolled to one side and his mouth slightly open, sagging sideways, breathing softly without snore. The gun had fallen gently to one side, though still held by the crook of the supporting arm.

The rat ran along the foot of the stack again, and came rustling up the hay, not ten feet from the man's head. Its little ferret eyes saw the sleeping form and it was inquisitive. It scurried a little nearer, with long nose working, an urgent expression on its evil face. Then, scenting the man smell, it dived into the shadow and was lost.

Far away a village clock chimed three, and the faint sound came on the breeze, but did not wake the sleeping man whose brain was busy with troublesome dreams. How constant are those ancient grey towers that brood with a paternal air over their respective hamlets! Like old family doctors, they seem to know the weaknesses and the lives of the villagers, and all through the march of the seasons they keep watch and ward. Beneath their shadows they group the new dead and the long dead, they see the whole story of many a humble life from the font to the grave under the nettles and wild hemlock, where the whitethroat bubbled in the summer hours. Squire and peasant, they gather them all, and chime on down the centuries, sunlight and starlight, all the same. . . .

A throttled "baa" awoke Johnson, and in an instant he was on one knee, peering into the darkness, his gun at the ready. A slight quickening of breath told of his hammering heart. He heard the sound of rumbling feet as sheep stampeded. Some were trying to leap the hurdles, others rushed up and down, bounding and bouncing in terror. Then a hurdle crashed flat and the whole flock came pouring through the gap, out into the field. The peewits lifted and went screaming in jerky circles as the tornado of terrified animals went scurrying among the ant-hills. Johnson slipped out of the hay without a sound, every nerve tense; he could make out nothing in the dim light. Now the sheep were running up the other end of the field; he could hear the rumble of their flying feet. Then, all was silent, and the man stood still. Suddenly, there came a sound that made the hair bristle on the back of his neck. It was a terrible throttled rattle, half-moan, half-sigh. He went forward with infinite caution, the butt of the gun ready in his shoulder, eyes straining towards the glimmering pales of the hurdles.

Lying on its side, with back legs still kicking feebly, was a sheep, a dark stain welling from under the neck. Johnson stood trembling, looking all about him, but the killer had vanished. The sound of the running sheep stopped, and only the complaining peewits were circling above him, though he could not see them. Oh! for a little more light, for a mere gleam of moon. . . . He could see nothing, and had left his torch in the stack. He went back to the stack and stood under its shadow, pulses still hammering, and mouth dry. What a fool to drop asleep . . . still the killer might come back . . . he would wait. Out in the field the sheep, still bunched together, were moving daintily, stopping ever and again with uplifted heads.

The minutes passed: ten, fifteen, half an hour, an hour. . . . Then his ears caught a faint sound coming from the direction of the dead sheep. Something was eating and tearing . . . the killer had come back! With trembling fingers he pushed the catch of the powerful torch and the vivid rays shot a beam through the blackness, illuminating the hurdles and the body of the sheep. Something dark was standing by the head, and two red, baleful eyes glowed like some gigantic moths, straight at the man. Then they slid sideways and Johnson saw the slim form of a fox, and, though he could not see it, a fox with one ear. . . .

When the Hazelbeech church clock struck three, Rufus was crossing the railway from the direction of Hieaway Wood. He turned up the slope of the hill and set his mask for Penny Plain. He had not killed and was hungry, and the Coldhangar rabbits might be worth a visit. He ran with effortless ease, with more of a slow, loping gait than a run, and his eyes and ears were telling him all he wanted to know. By the root of a wild crab another fox had been, a Creaton fox by the smell, and after investigating for some two minutes, Rufus went on up the high ridge of Penny Plain, intending to cut across to Coldhangar.

It was then he heard the sound of stampeding sheep and the wakeful peewits giving tongue. Something indeed was amiss. He stopped with lifted pad, listening with all his ears, his eyes no longer slits, but wide open. He heard the throttled cry of the murdered sheep, and then the sound of something coming across the field between the ant-hills. It came with some noise, and panting breaths, and Rufus slipped like a streak down the ditch. As he did so, some large, dark creature came under the five-barred gate and went on down the valley towards Hieaway. It was again quiet on Penny Plain, the sheep had ceased to stampede, though they were still in a solid mass one end of the field.

Rufus slipped under the roots of a blackthorn, and went loping across the field where the haystack loomed like the roof of a cottage in the far corner. Here there came to Rufus's nostrils the warm smell of blood, fresh blood, and it was good. So he stole forward, stopping every now and then until he came to the hurdles. There lay the still warm body on the trampled, muddy ground, among the half-hollowed turnips. And he began to eat his fill. . . .

Then, as we have seen, came the sudden glare of a great eye, which for a second paralysed him. But only for a moment. With his mask still red with the sheep's blood, he turned swiftly, and the great eye went out. A second later a stab of flame jabbed the darkness—two stabs—one, two, BANG! BANG! and the shot went whistling among the hurdles, sending the splinters flying and thudding into the muddy ground. One number three pellet sang through his erect ear like a great hornet, another laid open the back of his hind leg, but did not splinter the bone. The shock and pain seemed like the blow of a red-hot mallet, and for a second Rufus rolled over. But he was on his feet in an instant, streaking for the hedge. Two more shots rang out behind, and he heard the sigh of the slugs as they sped outwards over the field, but he was not waiting for any more. He ran swiftly for Coldhangar and the shelter of his earth.

He spent the next day licking his back leg. It was a difficult place to get at, and he had to sit like a cat with the wounded leg straight up in the air. As for the wound, it was only a flesh wound and soon healed, but now there was a price on his head with a vengeance. For he was branded, absurd as it was to naturalists and hunting men, as the Killer, and it behoved him to walk warily and circumspectly.

And Man sought to end his bright life.

Chapter Fourteen
SNOW IN THE FOREST

*Clap of a pigeon in winter spinney,
New-dropped lambs and a horse's whinney,
Crowing pheasant and cockerel's crow,
Elfin rustle of falling snow.*

THERE must have been some connection with the visit of Mr. Johnson to the kennels, and the coming of the hounds to Coldhangar and Hieaway, within a few days of each other. Weird and wonderful tales were going about of a fox the size of an Alsatian, that was killing full-grown sheep. Even the children became afraid to go to school, unless their fathers fetched them, but it was all needless fuss.

Though the farmer spent many another night under the haystack of Penny Plain, he never saw the killer again, or heard him, for that matter, and some said it was dead; perhaps a stray shot had wounded it, and it had died. Then, two days before Christmas, a single ewe was killed near the crossing spinney, and on Boxing Night seven sheep at Willow Tree Farm, almost under the farm windows. Bloodhounds were procured, and they took the trail of the killer straight over the railway up to Jackman's farm. Jackman, alarmed and with a horrid suspicion dawning in his mind, watched that night and found his cur had gone. It returned just before dawn with its muzzle dyed red, and Jackman shot it in the yard, and told nobody. The cur was missed, and soon the whole thing leaked out. But after that, no more sheep were killed, and Rufus was absolved from blame.

This was lucky, because the hounds had been worrying him. Two weeks running they had chased him, once from Coldhangar to Maidwell Dales where they lost the scent in the reeds, and could not find it again, and once from Hieaway, where they lost the scent on foiled ground near Naseby. Both runs had been dull, patchy affairs and are not worth noting here.

Rufus seemed destined to lose his mate each year, they killed his vixen in Old Poors Gorse, the scene of many a kill for Rufus's ancestors, and two of his cubs suffered the same fate. The third was shot by a farmer in mistake for a rabbit when ferreting, a genuine mistake.

The urge to wander came to him again in February, and he took himself off to Summermoon to find a new wife. He found changes. . . . The woodcutters had been busy, and a great many noble trees were gone and the pitiful havoc was sad to see. In every ride there were deep ruts from the tumbrils; mud, mud everywhere, and fallen, untidy sticks and tangles. Fresh-severed boles, raw and clean-looking; vivid chips scattered where once great trees had stood. The bramble bushes laid waste (no more starring dog-rose) and everywhere the signs of brutal handiwork. So he went on into Badby Woods, untouched as yet, still serene, and here he settled down to spend the rest of the winter.

There were plenty of foxes and he made a great enemy of an old warrior, a six-year-old dog-fox, who lived the life of a hermit under a great oak. They used to meet sometimes in their nightly huntings, and mighty battles were fought, Rufus usually getting the worst of the encounters. As the clicketing season approached and the vixens began to call for their mates, the old fox forsook his oak and went wife-hunting. It was inevitable, perhaps, that the two should meet when paying court to the same vixen, and Rufus had the greatest fight of his life.

It was at the full moon, and one night Rufus, hearing the siren call of a shameless hussy coming from Beddows' spinney in the valley, went over to pay his respects. He found her, in the moonlight, playfully rousing his old enemy to a frenzy of passion. The old warrior heard Rufus and winded him, and for a moment the two silent foxes regarded one another like graven statues. Then Rufus came slowly forward, treading delicately like a cat, the tip of his brush twitching and his single ear standing up in the moonlight like a shark's fin. Three feet from his enemy he stopped, and still the old fox did not move. Meanwhile, the vixen had drawn off a few paces, and had lain down, her feminine instincts glorying in the spectacle of two champions about to fight for her.

It was a dramatic scene, those two silent, tense figures, strung like arrows at the bow-string, ready to fly at each other's throats in the moonlit ride; and the mischievous lady, the cause of it all, sitting with lolling tongue, watching them. Overhead the giant trees were traced against the luminous sky, and the clear moon rode like a lighted port-hole in the star-dusted immensity of space. It was the old fox that moved first. To say that he moved would be wrong—he came like a bullet from a gun, and Rufus skipped aside like a boxer. Then he was round in a flash, his teeth meeting in empty air, just above the old fox's shoulder.

Now they were at it, snapping and parrying, all over the ride, rolling in the muddy wallows and smearing their coats with filthy water. Rufus drove the old beast back under the bushes until his stern came against a fallen log. Finding himself at bay, the older fox fought back with desperate fury, and got hold of Rufus's brush. The noise then was hideous, snarls of fury, yelps of agony, and blood everywhere. Rufus had the advantage of youth, and he made the most of it. He drove his enemy back slowly, yard by yard, fighting every inch of the way. Suddenly the old fox turned tail and bolted, growling and muttering, and went off to lick his sores. Rufus, his blood still up, pursued his vanquished enemy vindictively for over two fields. Then he went back for the vixen and found her gone. He trailed her into Fawsley Park, and came on her by the lake side, eating a moor-hen. She affected to ignore him as he came up, and went on crunching brittle bones, but when Rufus fawned over her she did not drive him away; she even gave him some of her kill. When dawn came they went happily away together and slept under a wood-pile in a ride.

Towards four o'clock in the afternoon it began to snow, first soft, wandering flakes feeling their way through the leafless trees, straying softly about and settling lightly on the wood-pile, melting at first, then lying, white on white, until the dark, wet logs were transformed. When Rufus came out from under the pile, the ride was white, and the windward side of the trees white to the topmost branches. Very soon the snow thickened into weaving patterns that shut out the distances. Tired birds, coming in to roost, flew low and moithered, and the sky grew dark and leaden. And all that night it snowed and snowed, and the wind rose and made a murmur in the trees.

Rufus went a-hunting and made a good kill. Some partridges, huddled all together in a covey by the side of a lonely rick, were stalked successfully. Rufus killed two birds, and their blood made little red holes in the snow. One bird he ate, and the other he carried to his wife in the wood-pile.

When dawn came it still snowed and the wind was rising. The flakes were not large now, but powdered like fine dust. Where the ride was exposed by a gap in the forest, the wind swept it into drifts, great carved mounds of virgin whiteness, on which could be traced the little footmarks of the birds running here and there in all directions. And still it snowed and snowed. The woodpile, a short while ago so distinct and black, was now but a mound of white, and the tracks of the foxes were plainly visible leading in under the heap. But it was warm enough inside, and all that bitter day the foxes slept warmly under the roof of snow-laden logs.

The hungry rabbits, intent on barking the young forest trees, left plain tracks that showed their every action, and round the rickyards the birds gathered in thousands—finches, blackbirds,

The earth was white

thrushes and crows. Some of the woodland trees could not bear their white weight, but shed great lumps that dunched softly when the wind stirred in the branches. And the grey wood-pigeons resorted to the allotments round the hamlets, stuffing themselves with the tops of the greens and running the risk of the villagers' crazy guns. At night they sought the thick fir trees; and the more exposed parts of the woods where they usually roosted were deserted.

And still it snowed, and snowed, and snowed. . . . All traffic on the roads was brought to a standstill and the wind carved great bastions of powdery snow on the high places. Some of the lonelier villages were isolated and supplies had to be carted by sledge, a thing unheard of, even in the memory of the oldest inhabitants. The wandering flakes, settling on the fur of Rufus as he emerged from the wood-pile, melted into beads of water. As he padded slowly along down the sheeted ride, his feather-weight scarce broke the surface, but his brush just touched the snow ever and again, leaving little wavy lines.

The poor blackbirds and fieldfares, puffed to twice their size, and with eyes that lacked the fullness of alert fear, hopped along hedgerows, and some were easy to catch—they were so weak.

In hard weather the feathered folk suffer terribly, for their only source of food, the green earth, is inches deep under the cruel crust, and at the end of the winter all the berries, or most of them, have been devoured. Round every spring in the fields, where the water was moving too fast to freeze, flocks of finches gathered, and along the spring below Henton's farm, the snipe came in in dozens.

Then were the white slopes of Merry Hill loud with laughter of the tobogganers, and the warm breath of live things puffed like kettles on the frosty air. After the third day the snow ceased, but resumed again on the fifth. In the parks and gardens the cedar branches crashed to the ground, and many a noble tree was spoiled. Rufus, hunting down a ride in Badby, saw and heard almost half of a great Canadian pine come down, and the white, muffled forest echoed to the roar of its fall, a sound that sent many wild things running for their holes.

Yet, on the whole, compared with the other creatures of the woods, the foxes did well, living almost entirely on rabbits and weakened birds. The rabbits, unable to get at the grass, hunted all the likely spots where they might bark the young saplings, and it was here Rufus and his wife got many a meal. The stoats, perhaps, suffered least, for that little gentleman, a mighty hunter always, can usually see that the inner stoat is satisfied, and tracking was even easier in the snow.

At last the sky cleared, and a quick thaw came that filled the rivers and streams to overflowing. Then was the land loud with the voice of many waters, and broad-bosomed floods spread out along the valleys in which the dying sunset skies were reflected. What a joy it was to see the first green patch of grass again, how sweet and purified the air became! And the woodland thrushes, no longer puffed and torpid, sang until you would have thought they would burst their throats. Down by the brook the flooded fields made great lakes where lonely haystacks stood, the tops of the surrounding rails just visible above the waters. The corpses of rabbits and hares were everywhere, and the foxes had many a meal.

It was towards the end of February that Rufus had another great run from the hounds, and added yet another store of experiences which were docketed for future use. On the twenty-third of February, hounds met at Badby on a warm, grey morning, with a southerly wind. It was one of those days when scent is good, but not superbly so, just enough to give Rufus a pretty run for his money. The night before he had dined well off a pheasant, stalked and killed in the open on the outskirts of the wood as it quested for hidden acorns under the oaks. So Rufus slept soundly (alone that night, for the vixen was elsewhere), in the wood-pile by the side of the ride.

He heard the sound of horses first (the field was in the centre of the wood when hounds drew) and he slipped away without fuss for Fawsley. There was ice on the lakes, but so thin it would scarce bear a moor-hen's weight, and there was to be no repetition of the tragic morning when five gallant couple of hounds went to their watery grave. The Huntsman saw him go and soon the chase was up; the same old music, now grown familiar, dogged his footsteps.

He set his mask for Sharman's Hill and the Hellidon Hills. He crossed the Chipping Warden road with a good lead. Hounds checked here, and Rufus gained a lot of ground, so much so that the sound of pursuit died and he thought he had shaken them off. How he disliked this glaring light of day where every fold in the ground, every ditch, had to be made the most of. Every bird seemed an enemy, shouting the way he had gone, swooping at him and halloaing him away.

Now the hounds began to filter through the hedge from the road, and the Huntsman made a wide cast above the spot where the fox had slipped through. The road itself was a mass of riders; some had dismounted and were tightening girths, others chatted and gossiped, and the wise ones kept alert and watchful, watching the casting hounds. Finding no scent up above, the Huntsman brought the hounds below, and in a few moments they began to speak, rather uncertainly, to the patchy scent that led towards Sharman's Hill. Then the road began to empty and soon only a line of cars was left with their watching occupants. One man, in a thick, tweed coat and hat pulled well over his eyes, was watching the hunt through a pair of field-glasses.

Meanwhile, Rufus was unhurried, and loped along at his easy gait, making the most of every available cover. It seems strange sometimes, to foot people who follow the hounds, that the fox is so seldom seen. The streaming pattern of the chase, seemingly on the very tail of the fox, galloping riders and running rustics, all seem to be pursuing some invisible creature, and, to the watcher, it seems all rather ludicrous.

There was a lot of cold plough at the foot of Sharman's Hill, and Rufus made the most of it. Luckily there were no sneaking, sable rooks to give him away, and he went up a long wet furrow, the sticky earth, gummy from the thaw, galling between his toes. Out through a ragged bullfinch* on to a stubble field, where the larks rose before him with liquid bubblings and dropping flight. A kestrel, hovering like a kite against the soft, pearly sky, saw the running spot of red and swooped in a great arc, then, seeing what the creature was, zoomed up again with hardly a movement of his scythe wings, and lit in the branches of a stunted hedgerow oak. Here he sat until the hounds came, fifteen minutes behind Rufus, puzzling their way with the doggedness of stoats over the plough and into the yellow stubbles. A covey of partridges that had seen the hawk and were cowering in one corner of the field, rose with a whirr and glided over three fields before they lighted again, all at once, in a lifting-dropping action. Then they ran and stopped with erect heads, looking towards the bustle of the hunt.

Meanwhile Rufus trotted on, keeping away from the roads, and following the ditches. He came to a low, stone wall, an uncommon feature in this part of the country, and he leapt on top of this like a hill fox, and ran along for fifty yards before dropping down, not on the far side, but the same side. Instinct, or perhaps it was experience, told him that this was the right thing to do, and sure enough, when the hounds puzzled up the wall and came to the spot where he had jumped up, they went scrambling over and searched the meadow (a little green triangular place hedged round with thorns) on the far side.

Here there was another long check, and people stood about, their horses gently steaming, or walked gravely up and down to keep their mounts from chill. A wide cast on the far side proved, naturally, fruitless, and the Huntsman took hounds up in the opposite direction and tried higher up, but still no answer to the puzzled noses. It was Orator that found the line. Finding nothing on the far side of the wall, he went off on his own, like the wise old beast he was, and hit the scent fifty yards below, where Rufus had

*A close clipped hedge.

jumped down. Not waiting or stopping, he gave loud tongue, and went away at a fast pace down the side of the wall. Within the space of a few moments things began to move. The other hounds and the Huntsman, hearing the voice of Orator, came running back, and soon they were well down on his line once more.

But Rufus had gained a lot of ground, and was swinging right-handed for Badby again. He was in country he did not know, and this to a fox is always disquieting. The sounds of pursuit were far behind, and he did not hurry himself. So he lolloped along, stopping ever and again to listen, until he came to the foot of Byfield Hill. . . .

Chapter Fifteen
THE HAPPY LIFE

Insect choirs at height of noon,
The small quiet sounds beneath the moon,
Querulous talk of a White Leghorn,
Cheep of mice among the corn.

WHEN Rufus reached the angle of a hedge at the foot of the hill, a lot of fieldfares and redwings were feasting on the berries. When they saw the fox they all flew away, "chuck, chucking," as they went. He sat down by a ditch and looked round, his one ear cocked inquisitively and his slits of eyes puzzling out a problem. The country seemed deserted. In the next field some horses were peacefully grazing, but this was the only sign of life.

Rufus raised his front pad and licked it carefully (it was the pad that bore the scar of the snare), then he sat upright like a cat and curled his brush round him. A solid phalanx of starlings came over a hedge and lit in the field in front, where they at once began to feed busily, quarrelling all the time because they are jealous birds, and hate seeing their fellows finding any tit-bits. All of a sudden Rufus saw the horses with their heads up, no longer feeding, but watching something near the ground. A second later a fox slipped through the opposite hedge, and came straight across the field to where Rufus was sitting. From the look of him he was not a beaten animal, and still carried his brush high, though he was mud to the elbows. He never saw Rufus, sitting against the red-brown tangle of the hedge, but slipped through a gap about a hundred yards above, and skirted the base of Byfield Hill. He had come from the Bicester country, and was heading for Badby, whither Rufus himself was bound.

The horses in the far field had continued to graze again, and a rook wandered over, not thirty feet above Rufus's head. He seemed to be swimming slowly through the soft, grey air, oaring himself along with his sheeny, blue wings, the fingers of which were spread wide with every down-thrusting motion. He was an old bird with a very bald face and a big knob on the base of his pick-axe bill (he had been born seven years before in Byfield Rookery), and ever and again he rose in the air and said, "Caw-caw-caw" in a rather rich and musical voice. He never saw Rufus under the berried hedge, so he went on and on, until he was a mere wandering speck that melted into the soft blues of distance.

Rufus trotted down the hedge until he came to the trail of the strange fox and sniffed the scent. He recognised it, for this same fox had left his card in Summermoon two months before, and Rufus had even had a minor fight with him over a vixen. Having satisfied his curiosity, Rufus turned round and went at a leisurely lope for Badby, keeping to the ditches and hedgerows, and making the most of every little spinney. Behind him, the horses began to be restless, for they saw a single galloping rider in pink cantering down the slope of a field, and some sheep were running and bunching. Soon there came other horsemen, and the whimper of a hound. The kestrel, that had watched the hunt go by, 'way back on the trail of Rufus, saw a strange sight. Two packs of hounds, racing towards one another, and two fields converging. The Bicester and the Pytchley, both intent on killing their fox.

Soon the hounds of the former pack came pouring through the hedge at the foot of Byfield Hill, and almost at the same moment the Pytchley Hounds came through the corner of the same field on the trail of Rufus. It was an unusual sight as the two packs mingled and the fields behind were black and red with horsemen, an enormous gathering. They came to the place where the fox trails crossed, and Rufus's being the fresher, and not so spent as the much-run fox's, they all came after Rufus, who was now taking things very easily nearly a mile and a half away, on his way back to Badby. . . .

Soon he quickened his pace, making for Righton Hill rising above the clustering oaks. On this side of the county, the fields are inclined to be small, for it is on the verge of Warwickshire with its little meadows hedged around with trees. He skirted the hill, and saw the line of Badby Woods and shelter, over a rim of withered grass. Along several plough lands he went, over a little brook, doubled back and along the brook, then across a wide meadow foiled with sheep—and he was in the woods.

Behind, the pursuit was dead.

Hounds had been manœuvred into a barn; the lengthy business of sorting had begun; and people were jogging homewards.

Against a pale, soft sky, the pigeon hosts were streaming in to roost, and many thrushes were singing of the spring. Rufus went back to his wood-pile, rather tired, and found his vixen awaiting him. Down the ride, the long puddles in the ruts reflected the quiet colours of the dying sky, and the trees stood without a tremor of a branch, for the wind had died away. It was all very peaceful, and it was good to rest, no more baying hounds or thrum of hooves, no more music of the pure-toned horn floating behind him. Only the clear singing of the woodland choirs.

And to Rufus the woods had been always kind, offering shelter and security and a tuneful peace, providing him with game, and a home for his family, and a haven from mankind. Little wonder that he came to regard the woods as his greatest friend and ally, a shield against the terrors of the day. When the light had died and the last glimmer drained from the puddles, he came out of the wood-pile and, with his vixen, set his mask for his old haunts. In his mind were the tangled thickets of Coldhangar and Blueberry, and the caressing wind in the Hieaway firs.

As they went along, hunting in their journey, the moon climbed the sky and threw dark shadows from their stealthy forms. It cast great interlacing shadows from the hedgerow trees, from oak, and ash, and elm. And the white mist lay in swathes on the low ground, smelling raw and cold to their sensitive noses. Near Holdenby Mill the vixen caught a moor-hen that was roosting in a low willow, and together they ate it, happily, in the moonlight.

It was a fairy place, with the silhouette of the mill like a misty castle rising above the talking stream. Rufus went into the miller's garden to investigate, because there was a strong smell of rabbit. He crossed the potato patch with the withered haulms lying about, and passed a hen-run that was caked and shiny by the tramplings of the prisoners. Standing against the mill outhouse was a large box, and resting on this a smaller box with a wire front. Here the miller's little boy kept his prize rabbits, poor, foolish creatures whose only life was to hop up and down the wire, and stand up on their hind legs and nibble cabbage stalks through the wire. They were rarely cleaned out and the hutch stank of ammonia. Rufus sat below, looking up at the hutch for a second or two, and then gathered himself for a spring.

He landed lightly on a projecting ledge close to the end of the hutch, and he could hear the rabbits thumping in alarm in the enclosed portion of their box. Meanwhile, the vixen had come up across the garden and was sitting on her haunches below, watching him interestedly. Rufus tried to scratch a way into the hutch through the wire, but only cut his pads, and the narrow ledge offered no purchase. Then the vixen leapt up beside him, and together they scratched at the box, moving it ever so slightly towards the edge. It suddenly heeled and crashed to the ground on its side, the terrified rabbits being thrown on top of one another and kicking wildly. Scared, the foxes retreated behind the cabbages, because the noise had been loud in the silence of the misty night, but no window was thrown open, no dog barked, only the mill-stream went talking on, in an undertone, to itself.

Inside the overturned hutch the rabbits were huddled in a corner, with their tails outwards, and their silly eyes staring into the angle of the box. They were breathing quickly, too, and their poor little hearts pumped rapidly. Finding all was quiet, the foxes stole across to the hutch and began working at the wire. Soon they had scratched a big hole and Rufus pushed inside and killed the rabbits, but not before he had received a slashing stroke from the hind claws of one terrified buck. He dragged the body of one of them out through the wire and the vixen helped him eat it. He went into the hutch again, and came out with another, which he carried away into the cabbages and buried clumsily in the dark, soft soil.

Then they went on up the bank of the stream, full fed and content, and as dawn was greying in the east they lay up for the day in a thicket of willow and dead reeds close to the brook. They slept undisturbed all through the hours of daylight, and when evening came continued their way northwards until Rufus came into his own country where he had been bred and born. And he took his vixen to Hieaway, to the earth where he had been suckled as a cub, in the sand bank under the singing firs.

During the following night they hunted across to Coldhangar and a mighty wind was roaring through the trees. Coldhangar was turbulent with mighty sound; the fierce gusts tore through the bare tree tops and set the ash poles rocking and clashing as they swung like pendulums this way and that. The poor wood-pigeons were forced to come down into the blackthorn, and the bushes were thick with the portly grey bodies.

Rufus killed a rabbit by the ash poles and took it back to his wife. The latter was now big with young and was searching for a warm earth. She was a difficult lady to please, and of late had begun to be temperamental and changeable, like all ladies, and poor old Rufus got many a snap when he was trying to be helpful. But she eventually decided on Hieaway, and one night she went down into the earth and would not let Rufus come near her. He went off miserably by himself, and had a bad night's hunting, returning in the greying dawn to the crest of dark firs.

Strange smells were in the earth and a growling mother; there were also baby noises, suckings and tiny whimpers that told Rufus another family had been born to him, but he was not allowed inside the earth, and he hardly dared to show his nose. He slept during the day in the box bushes close at hand and went off early in the evening to Old Poors Gorse, where I am sorry to say he found an unattached and attractive vixen, that took up a lot of his time—time that should have been spent in hunting for his family. Just after three in the morning he finished with her, and the fires of his passion being quenched, went over to the Hawking Tower and killed two runner ducks. He buried one, after eating a little of the breast, and took the other back to Hieaway. It was a long trek and his neck ached throbbingly by the time he reached the wood.

He found the vixen outside the earth in petulant mood. She took the duck from him and began to tear it up. She did, however, relent a little, and licked her husband on the nose. He lay down then smiling at her with his mask set in a grin, but still he was not allowed in the earth where three mouse-coloured objects squirmed and burrowed in the warm fur of their mother.

However, the earth was no place for male intrusion, and the vixen was following her natural instincts. Rufus was just as much in the way as a human father is at such times, and he had the same sense of wonderment and perplexity at all this bother and fuss and strange, new smells.

The next night he went again to Old Poors Gorse to look for his lady friend, but she was not there. He trailed her to Blue Covert, but could not find her. So in the moonlight he went on along the railway, passing Hieaway to the left, until he came to the water meadows where, as a cub, he had come that summer night now so long ago, when he escaped from the stable of Wildwoods. He went up the hill, through the withy beds and the line of shrubs, until he was close to the house. The drive was full of cars, gleaming monsters that winked back at the moon, and from the lighted windows came the strains of music, for Pamela was having a dance.

He crossed the lawn, past the lily pool and the lead cherub blowing down a conch shell, and crept under the shrubberies. Then he came into the stable yard, and sniffed under the crack of the door where once he had been held a prisoner. There was a horse within, and it smelt and heard Rufus, and its eyes rolled round as it mumbled a strand of hay.

Rufus was just going on into the kitchen garden, when suddenly, a door opened and a stream of light shot across the gravel.

"Look! what's that running along the wall?" he heard Pamela's voice. "Looked like a cat to me!" said a man's rather drawling voice. . . . "No, it was a fox, I'm sure, just by the stable there." . . . "Oh, never mind the beastly fox, fancy talking of foxes with a moon like that . . . look at it, Pam . . . it's like a summer night." . . .

Rufus went on down through the cabbages, there was hunting to be done.

Chapter Sixteen
THE TRAP

The titmouse crying his wares to sell,
Ringing his fairy muffin bell;
Snuffling hedgehog's nightly prowl,
Quavering cry of a hunting owl.

O LD Mr. Bumpus, the gardener at Wildwoods, was setting a rabbit trap by the fence of the kitchen garden. About ten yards out in the field was a refuse heap where the house waste was thrown, and he had noticed several rats using the run under the wire. As he straightened his back and surveyed his handiwork, the neatly hidden jaws innocently spread and the few dead leaves which entirely hid it from view, he heard light steps coming down the cinder path. It was Pamela, hatless as always, her dark hair clustering at the nape of her neck, as thick and glossy as a spaniel's, and a basket in her hand.

"Good morning, Bumpus. Where can I find some daphne? Mummy wants some for the house as we're having a little dance to-night and I'm doing the flowers."

"Good mornin' to 'ee, Miss. Why, yes, to be sure, there's some under the west wall yonder, though your Ma 'as 'ad it near all, but there's a wee bit left. And, oh, Miss, will ye see Peter don't come nigh the fence, there, as I've set a trap for an ole rat I seed these last few mornin's—they come to the waste 'eap in the medder, an' the master says I was to cotch 'im if I could. 'Ere ye are, Miss, there 'e be, under them leaves . . . see 'im? Reckon that'll cotch 'im next time 'e comes."

Pamela went down on one knee by the fence, and looked at the withered leaves so cunningly arranged. As she knelt there, her dark hair falling forward round her finely moulded cheeks and white pillar of neck that showed above her jumper, old Bumpus thought what a fine young leddy she was to be sure. Like all the other servants, he liked her unaffected friendly ways . . . "a true leddy, to be sure, not like a lot o' these young things about that treated you like dirt." . . .

"But where, Bumpus? I can't see it. Show me, please. You must be very clever to hide it so well."

"Why, there, to be sure, Miss. Right under your very nose, Miss, under them leaves." The old man chuckled. "Ah reckon if you can't see un, the old rat won't."

"Oh! There. . . . I see it now. . . . Does it kill the rat right out?"

"Lor' bless you, yes, Miss . . . like that." . . . The old man cracked his thumb and finger.

Pamela looked up and saw his creased, brown hand, like a mole's, with its broad, stubby fingers. "Well, I hope it does, I can't stand seeing an animal suffer. Yes, I'll see Peter doesn't come in the garden, and I'll tell Mummy, too."

She got to her feet and went off down the path with a slow easy walk, the walk of a good horsewoman. . . .

Rufus went down through the cabbages . . . there was hunting to be done. He came to the fence and stopped; he thought he caught the taint of man smell somewhere, and there were foot-marks in the soft, dark soil by the rhubarb. Then he began to squeeze under the fence. . . .

There was a curious snap right under his chest . . . and a shaft of hot fire darted through his foreleg, the same leg that had got caught in the snare. He leapt back, snarling, but a cruel jerk brought him almost on his nose, and a chain moved like a metal snake among the leaves. . . . He was held fast, trapped, by the iron jaws. . . .

He lay half on his side, hidden by the rhubarb stalks, biting at the steel until it was bright. The cruel teeth had pierced the flesh and bit deeply into the tendons of the leg, and every movement was agony. He pulled the loose chain out with his teeth and laid it in a loop on the soil, then, with his free paw he scraped earth over it. Still he was held . . . this agony . . . this fear. His vixen waiting in Hieaway, the dark firs whispering and the night rustles in the scented bushes. . . . An owl hooted. . . . From the house came the strains of music and the laughter of men and girls, distant hand-clapping. . . . If only he could rid himself of this cruel thing that held him.

The clear moon shone down serenely, though it was dark under the rhubarb leaves, which spread like umbrellas above him. He could hear and smell a rat coming through the wire and little squeaks came from the garbage heap in the field . . . and the smell of potato peelings and earth. . . . From the house the sound of music stopped, for the dancers were thronging the buffet and the buzz of conversation seemed like a choir of chattering starlings. . . .

"Crunch, crunch." The white teeth worked away at the steel, and the light from the moon began to wheel under the rhubarb. In the stables a hunter was kicking his stall, and at every kick Rufus ceased to bite, and lay still with only his heart pounding. . . . Now the music began again, muted and muffled, for a window had been closed, and it was not so loud as before. . . .

How still the tall limes stood against the greenish sky, what a world of stars above! He should be away now beyond Coldhangar, stalking the rabbits as they scuttled in the moonlight, or went, bob-bobbing down a ride . . . instead he was here held fast, to be done to death when the light came . . . would it never come? . . . Exhausted he lay passive, his one ear alert for every sound and his eyes half closed. There were sounds now of singing: "For auld lang syne . . . For auld lang syne, should auld acquaintance be forgot." . . . Laughter, the sudden throbbing murmur of a car, someone revving up an engine, squeals of laughter and the sound of feet crushing gravel. He heard a car roar off down the drive, then another, the bray of a horn. . . . After a while the sounds began to die . . . one last car roaring away through the night, sending a glare on the bare tracery of the lime trees. Shutting doors and windows, a sudden leap of reddish light behind an upper curtained window . . . Marley church striking four. . . .

Suddenly he heard something coming down the path of the kitchen garden, and he caught the reek of dog. Peter, escaping from his round basket in the kitchen, had been out visiting a lady friend who lived in Marly, and was now filling in the time, and his stomach, until the doors should be opened in the morning. When he got near the rhubarb (he was on his way to an orgy in the waste heap) he caught the whiff of fox and stopped. . . .

"Yes, no mistaking it, and close, too . . . this must be investigated." . . . He came down the path slowly, then stopped. Something dark was lying under the spreading leaves. . . . "Grrrrrrrrrrrrrrrrrrrrrrrrrrrrr!"

Pamela was lying awake, staring at the tracery of the bare trees that rose like a Japanese print across the square of the open window. A wonderful night for February . . . as Stephen said . . . almost like a summer night. . . . Stephen . . . he had tried to kiss her and he did not really love her . . . rather a silly ass. . . . Now she felt unhappy, out of tune with everything . . . out of tune . . . that described it. And then he had kissed her, savagely, and he smelt just a little of whisky, she remembered. . . . Oh, what was the use of it all? . . . Stephen . . . who cared only for a good time, and hunting, and playing about with girls . . . never anything worth while. . . . With a fierce gesture she threw back the bed-clothes and went to the window.

The garden lay bathed in mysterious light, like a setting for Midsummer Night's Dream that she had seen last year in Town . . . Gielgud as Oberon. . . . Lovely, lovely. . . .

A sudden crescendo of yaps from the end of the garden. . . . Good Heavens, Peter was out . . . the trap! . . .

She clutched her dressing-gown off the door, and slipped her feet into her fur slippers. . . . Yes, that was it, he must have got out of the kitchen under cover of all the bustle and excitement and gone down to the ash pit. . . . The little beast, it served him right. . . .

The floor of the hall was strewn with cigarette ends and paper streamers, torn and crumpled; there was a smell of stale scent and food. . . . She let herself out of the back door, nervously eyeing the cockroach which scurried blackly, like some indecent thing, along the wainscoting . . . a turn of the key and she was out in the chilly night and moonshine. Desperate sounds from the kitchen garden—growls, yelps of agony, scufflings.

She ran like a deer down the long walk, her shadow black and flying with her . . . down past the lead cherub and the twinkle of the moonshine in the water of the lily pool, through the little iron gate, and into the kitchen garden. . . .

Rufus heard and saw the white Highland belly-crawling towards him in the moonlight, and faced round to do battle. He was terribly handicapped by the trap, but he would fight, he would fight.

The terrier came all at once in a rush of fury and Rufus met him with a slashing snap. But the terrier was on top of him, and they rolled under the rhubarb until a jerk of agony pulled Rufus away from the slavering jaws, and in a flash he bit his antagonist across the neck until the terrier yelped with agony. And then came Pamela, wide-eyed and angry. She saw the black and white forms rolling and writhing, biting and snarling, and for a moment she thought Peter had a rat under the fence.

And then she saw the fox, lying half on its side, snarling and showing its white teeth. She caught the frantic Peter by the collar, and his wild yelpings were strangled in his throat. She got the belt from her dressing-gown and tied the excited terrier to the fence, and then she turned to Rufus. He lay, half in shadow and half in the moonlight, one side of his neck red with blood, and his poor, mangled foot stretched out in front of him, half-buried under the blood-bespattered leaves. His eyes were closed and he lay as still as death. For a second she looked at him, and then, a wave of infinite pity sent her to her knees beside him. She felt for the trap under the leaves and her fingers found the cruel spring. Very gently she released the crushed paw and pulled the body gently out from under the rhubarb. . . . That old brute Bumpus! The old BRUTE!

She picked the warm, furry body up in her arms and the head sagged limply, dripping beads of blood that smeared her blue silk gown. And then she saw the one single erect ear, the other was a mere ragged ridge and seemed infinitely pathetic. . . . This must be the fox she had heard such a lot about—Rufus, the one-eared fox. . . . Peter was nearly strangling himself with baffled rage and jealousy. She carried the limp body in her arms, holding it like a baby. In the kitchen was the basket where Peter should rightly be safely tucked up, and she laid the body on the old blanket.

Was the fox really dead? . . . She could not feel any movement under the fur, a slight tremor perhaps, a mere quiver of a dying nerve. . . . She had a wild idea of brandy. . . . Yes, she would pour some between his clenched teeth; there might be still some spark of life. She went into the dining-room, hating the signs of recent merry-makings, and took out the flask from the sideboard. Then she went into the scullery to get a teaspoon. The floor was crawling with beetles and she stepped fearfully, gathering up her night-gown above her slim, white ankles. Then, with a spoon in one hand and the flask in the other, she tiptoed back into the kitchen.

By the last dying embers of the fire lay the round basket, and inside the crumpled grey blanket, bearing on one corner a little stain of blood the size of a penny piece. But Rufus was not there.

She looked round the kitchen, wildly, under the sombre shadow of the dresser, the table. . . . In the scullery, only more black beetles. . . . Really cook should put down some borax. . . . No, he was gone. The back door had been left ajar, he must have gone out. . . . Well, the deceitful little sneak!

Pamela felt a feminine pang of anger against the ungrateful creature . . . shamming all the time. . . . Down by the fence, an outraged Peter was straining at his bonds, and as Rufus limped painfully on three legs down the valley, he heard the barkings suddenly cease. . . .

Chapter Seventeen
THE LAST SUMMER

The nightingale in the blackthorn brake,
Keeping the forest folk awake;
Twittering larks in the winter wheat,
The stealthy padding of secret feet.

THE March wind was playing a merry jest with the winter-weary world. Begone all signs of autumn's sadness and fallen leaves! Now for a real spring-clean of copse and meadow, street and town. The dead beech leaves, where the bramblings had hunted for mast when the year was old, whirled up and up on a long journey as exciting as that of a magic carpet, to come to a restless rest in the valley floor below Hazelbeech. Some lighted in the brimming stream and were carried nearly to Brampton Mill, some lit in a muddy gateway and were trampled into the soil, and strangest of all, perhaps, one red-brown beech-leaf was whirled into a passing lorry and carried all the way to Manchester. There, after many adventures, it was used by a robin for building its nest in a wall—truly, a much-travelled leaf!

The wind bustled the sable rooks over the crossing spinney, and weeded out all the weakly rotten trees that could not live through another green summer. And it swept the garden of Wildwoods clean, the old house sitting the gale like a securely anchored ship. Only the smoke was blown straight and whirling, as it ventured above the moulded lips of clustering chimneys. It blew the sparrows inside out, until they looked like broken umbrellas, and all the little useless twigs were combed out of the lime trees and lay scattered up the drive.

Pamela was daily abroad on Wendy, an unruly sable curl

blown athwart her cheeks, and the shiny grass rippling under the drumming hooves of her little mare.

You can imagine what a rushing and a roaring the firs made of it all, up in Hieaway Wood. Their dark, tasselled branches threshed and tossed like manes of hair, and all the old pigeons' nests were blown down. Pigeons are lazy birds, and use the same nest again and again because they simply will not be bothered to build a clean, new structure.

So Rufus's three children, lusty cubs now, were introduced to a fresh, new world which had undergone quite a renovation, where everything had been tidied up, seemingly for their special benefit. They would emerge from the earth towards evening, listening furtively to the wind roaring through the wood, and watch, puzzled, the fairy dance of the leaves on the sandy slope below the earth. Once, a fir-cone fell with a resounding thump right on top of one of the cubs and scared him out of his wits.

Rufus was dreadfully lame and his foot was never fully to recover from the effects of the iron trap. When dusk fell he would limp down the hill from Hieaway, rather a pathetic little halting shadow, which seemed so fearful of a lurking enemy. And this new handicap had a certain effect upon him; it made him hunt near to home and to become an experienced robber of hen roosts. Traps were set for him, but now some instinct always told him of the hidden danger, and poison, too, he seemed to sense and left it alone.

Towards the end of the month, the winter had one last spiteful stab, and the land was briefly white. Rufus, abroad earlier than usual from the reeds of Lamport ponds, raided a chicken-house near the Post Office. It was a bold thing to do because the light had not yet gone and people were still about in the roads. And the sequel served him right.

The chickens were housed within a high wall at the back of the Post Office, and in the bottom of the wall was a little opening through which the hens had access to the field. Finding all was quiet, Rufus slipped within this aperture unobserved, and killed three surprised hens before they could squawk. Then they all bundled through the hole in the wall and proclaimed loudly in the meadow that there was a murderer in the fowl-house. Rufus waited within the wall, as a cat waits for a mouse at a hole. Overhead was an ancient apple tree, and a tit saw him and called him all sorts of uncomplimentary names.

The postmaster happened to be away in the local county town and his wife was looking after the shop, otherwise the hens would have been driven in from the field long before, and the wooden door put over the hole to keep such persons as Rufus out. It was nearly half-past six when she remembered, and went into the field to call them. There in the snow were grouped the hens, all clucking and peering and gabbling like a lot of old women at a mothers' meeting. And when their mistress appeared they still remained out in the snow, and would not be driven in through the hole. This was, indeed, strange behaviour, so the woman went across to the yard and, suspicious, peeped inside.

Rufus, hearing approaching footsteps, fled to the shelter of the apple-tree bole, but his brush betrayed him, sticking out from behind the mossy bulge of the root. Mrs. Gabbins was a woman of resource; she immediately ran to the trap-door and barred the hole up. Rufus, darted for the trunk but his maimed paw gave no grip and after scrabbling wildly, he fell to earth, and crouched, snarling, behind the tree.

After securing the hole, Mrs. Gabbins ran back into the "shop" and sent a child running for old Mr. Ward, who lived in the cottage at the end of the road. He was digging in the dusk, and the reek of his blue shag was strong on the air. When the child delivered her message the old man went into his cottage, and got his big thorn stick with the knob on the end, which he had cut himself, as a boy, in Coldhangar spinney. Then he went hobbling down the road to the Post Office.

He found Mrs. Gabbins with her nose to the crack of the door leading into the hen-yard. Rufus was still crouched behind the tree, thinking the matter out. He knew a man would soon arrive, and it was lucky for Rufus that old Mr. Ward had not got a gun. He saw the door open and the figure of the man come through, armed with a big stick. Behind peered the eager, excited face of Mrs. Gabbins, and she was vaguely clutching a broom. The old man advanced on the fox with uplifted stick, his face tense and eager, and every muscle braced for a deadly cutting blow.

But Rufus was ready for him. He let the man get close to him and then went straight as an arrow between his legs. Mrs. Gabbins saw the fox coming and uttered a piercing shriek, dropping the broom and throwing her apron over her head. Rufus went between her legs, too, because she was in the way, and when old Ward, turning and cursing, saw the tail of Rufus disappear under the woman's skirt, he imagined dreadful things, and the wild shrieks of Mrs. Gabbins were also suggestive.

Rufus went straight through into the shop, knocked over a pile of Quaker Oat boxes, and slipped out into the street by the sitting-room window, which, luckily for him, was ajar. . . .

With the coming of April the danger of the hounds departed, and Rufus was safe, taking even chances, until the following year. This was indeed lucky for him, for had they run him when his paw was yet so stiff, he would not have travelled more than a couple of fields. But for all that, he had one very bad scare. It was in the second week in April. He had taken to kennelling in a pollard willow that grew over the stream about a mile above Brampton Mill. As it leant out over the water at a gradual angle, it was easy to climb, and in the top there was a nice warm hollow, windproof and cosy, where a fox might pass a very comfortable day. He had found this tree when hunting a rat. A little owl had to be evicted first, however, and the hollow was full of beetle pellets and wing cases, which interested Rufus because he ate beetles himself.

This bright spring morning, when the water sparkled in the clean sunlight and the first swallows were skimming the mill pool,

Rufus was sleeping deeply after a successful night's hunting below Spratton. He had killed a fine cockerel and was now sleeping off the effects in his dreams, and he slept as if he were a stud-bred fox. And then, suddenly, he was awake. And the sound was of the Great Fear, and he knew not what to do. Up the river, past the mill, came a stream of walking people carrying long poles. Some wore green coats and scarlet caps, and there was a goodly sprinkling of tweed-clad youths and maidens, Pamela among them. The otter hounds came up the river slowly searching every likely hole and root. They found the drag of an otter in the willow thicket close to the mill. It was the sound of their excited yelps that roused Rufus in his tree. He did not move, however, but lay curled round like a big red caterpillar, hoping the bustle and noise would pass by. But instead of going away, the sounds became more distinct, and in a short while the hounds came up to the tree. The air was full of exciting smells and sounds as the huntsmen and hounds splashed out in the shallow water. Every now and then one of the hounds would whimper, and the sound sent the hair bristling on the crouching fox's back.

Then there came scramblings of claws on the trunk of the tree and a moment later one of the hounds was looking down into the mouth of the hole. It could smell and see Rufus below, and immediately set up a great noise that drew the other hounds to the spot. One of the huntsmen climbed the tree and stirred up Rufus with the end of his pole. The fox bounded out with a snarl and ran through the people. One man hit at him with his pole, and Pamela saw that the fox was Rufus because he had only one ear. He made off as fast as he could, and was puzzled to find no hounds were after him.

In the bright spring sunshine the hunt went on up the stream towards Spratton station, where the new, white lambs ran with their portly mothers. As for Rufus, he went across to Hieaway and did not sleep in the willow tree again. . . .

As spring merged into another summer, Rufus's paw began to

give him less trouble, but the work of healing was slow and he still went with a slight limp. He was able to travel farther afield, however, and did not rely so much on man for a livelihood. A fox that takes to raiding hen roosts and village ash heaps deteriorates into a very poor sort of beast, and is soon killed. Rufus had learnt that man was his very worst enemy and would kill him at the first opportunity. Therefore, while game was plentiful at any rate, he would hunt his wild fields and woods and live the life of a good, clean fox. And a fox's world, it must be remembered, is not of our world. It is of the night and the stars and moon. It is under the night skies that he hunts for food, and love, and enjoyment. Maybe, in the first place, it was man that made him into a night-hunting animal, and this was the reason he, like the badger, had survived unto the present age of the world.

And he took his toll from the sleeping hosts of furred and feathered things. Occasionally, it is true, he caught rabbits (semi-nocturnal beasts), but chiefly sleeping birds and other creatures that fell to him. His ear was attuned to the voices of the night, to the steady rhythm of the quietened pulse and subconscious breath of sleeping life.

Sometimes he would stop in the dewy fields among the river mists and hear some distant reveller, merry with ale, carrolling his way along the high road. And the glaring searchlights of the cars, feeling like pencils of light the delicate tracery of green, hanging curtains of trees, alarmed him, and made him keep to the shadow of a ditch.

But the summer passed uneventfully for Rufus. Haytime came and went, and soon another harvest. Down the long walks of Wildwoods the big hollyhocks knotted up to flower, and the beds on the shaven lawns were gay with snapdragons. In the mothy dusk of many a summer night Rufus went there and caught mice under the lavender bushes in the kitchen garden. But, of course, nobody knew anything about it, only Peter would bark next morning, when he smelt the fox.

As to the family of cubs that played that day in Hieaway at the beginning of the year, all were now fending for themselves, and any still evening they would be playing about in the low-lying meadows below Hieaway Hill, catching beetles or moles (they did not always eat the latter as moles have a queer taste) and trying to stalk rabbits. . . .

To Rufus it still seemed (why should it not?) that life was a constant thing that would never end, and now he had lived for so long—so long. What joy indeed to roam the wide, rolling fields by Faxton and the Hawking Tower, where no hound came after through the starlit night! He knew each little talking brook, singing its way down the scented silent hours, each with its own song and its own tune. If only we could hear, as did Rufus, the sounds of the quiet night! The talking of streams and rivers, the breathing of many sleeping things, and of creatures, restless in their sleep. Like the sea, the streams were never silent, nor had been since Time began or ever the world was made; their voices were friendly, voices that wished him well and eternal life. Truly, then, it was a lovely world.

Chapter Eighteen
THE LAST CHAPTER

*This was his life. Then so shall he
Under the stars gain sanctuary;
There shall he find a peace again,
Rest from the hounds of the devil-men.
Fruitful his hunting to dim day's birth,
Sweet be his sleep in English earth.*

PAMELA, her collar-bone broken and a weal across one pink cheek, was sitting by the big west windows of Wildwoods, knitting (demurely) a yellow hunting waistcoat. It was hard luck, taking a toss just at the beginning of the season, and now she would be out of things for some time. But there were compensations. Attentive young men came bearing gifts to her couch of pain and each had to be dealt with in a different way, according to her instincts.

As she sat plying the clicking needles, Peter, the white Highland, was sitting up in the window seat, staring out into the sodden garden, already greying in the mists of a November afternoon. On top of the rose pergola a robin was perched, singing a sad little ditty to the passing year, but Pamela could not hear it because the window was closed against the damp air. Soon she laid down her knitting and looked through the mullioned panes to the misty valley. In the distance, almost on the edge of the far hill, stood the square tower of Marly Church, and the long, wooded ridge of the park.

Old Bumpus went along the gravel path wheeling a barrow, and from the bottom of the garden came a drift of blue smoke. Pamela saw him go down to the heap and take his two short boards that he used for lifting leaves, and start to empty the barrow. He dare not tip the heavy barrow sideways because it hurt his "back" and just now the lumbago was "summat crewel." Peter, his ears cocked, sat watching every movement of the old man, whining quietly to himself. From the top of the rose tree the robin dropped to the path, and sat awhile with cocked head, in the manner of a thrush listening for worms on a lawn.

As Bumpus heaped on more leaves the smoke grew dense, until the drift shut out the distant view in a whitey-blue veil of vapour. Two blackbirds came out from under the shrubberies and began to run about the lawn. When they moved they cocked up their tails and ran swiftly and smoothly, with beaks held low to the ground.

Now, old Bumpus was coming up the path, wheeling the empty barrow, and the robin flew up on to a twig just over his head and watched him go by underneath with side-cocked head. On the lawn the two blackbirds ran swiftly and took wing at the rumble of the barrow.

As Pamela continued to watch she saw a red virginia creeper leaf detach itself from above the window and rest for a moment on the ledge outside. Then it rustled down out of sight, sorrowfully, as if unsure of its mind. On the lime trees bordering the drive, several yellow round leaves were wagging as if they were waving good-bye to summer days. This brought to Pamela a train of thoughts, of people saying good-bye, waving good-bye. . . . Those Irish peasants at Killarney, seeing their boy off to America . . . the terrible grief in their eyes. . . . She remembered one old lady in particular, with a black shawl round her head, whose face had been graven in a dreadful smile and all the while the tears had been slowly trickling down her cheeks. There had been some vulgar tourists laughing and pushing at the same window as the boy, and they kept jostling him so that he had been hidden. Some hikers, in khaki shorts and berets were on the platform, and they, too, pushed the old woman and her husband. The old creatures had borne the roughness with blind patience, like cattle, only their yearning eyes filled with eagerness and utter misery. . . .

Outside, on the misty path, the robin was again hopping sideways, his merry little bead of an eye, that had earned him the friendship of mankind, peering fearlessly about him. . . .

And then, from out of the blue drifting reek of the bonfire below the lawn, Pamela saw Rufus. That sudden appearance was dramatic, and forgetting her shoulder, she sat upright in her chair and the knitting dropped to the floor. It was Rufus without doubt, and a Rufus that was in distress. The brush was down, dragging the wet grass, the back was bowed and the mask low, and he moved so wearily . . . so wearily. He went across the lawn into the shrubberies by the stable and was lost. . . .

Pamela sat without moving, eyes fixed on the lawn and drifting smoke, thinning now as a red core began to burn in the heart of the leaves. . . . Another blackbird came out on to the lawn and hopped about. He found a worm and tugged and tugged until it came out. Then he bent over it greedily and gobbled it. A beaten fox, the one-eared fox that had been caught in Bumpus's trap that night of the dance. . . . God! the hounds must not get him . . . it would be dreadful.

She got up from the chair and went out of the room. From the lobby she took her thick tweed coat and threw it round her shoulders and went out into the garden. Williams, the chauffeur, was washing down the Buick in the yard, and a hose spirted in his hand, the stream of water drumming loudly on the panels. She walked round the house past the shrubberies, out on the lawn, and stood listening. But all she heard was the sad little song of the robin, on the rose tree, and the air smelt raw and damp. No, it couldn't be . . . and yet . . . that was a beaten fox. . . . She went slowly back into the house.

She opened the window of the west room, and took up her knitting again. But it was no good, she could not work—something made her listen and watch. Now there was only just a faint reek of blue from the bonfire as the leaves had burnt to a white ash, powdery and fine. . . . And then, her heart leapt. On the far side of the valley, below Marly church, she saw two horsemen, far away, galloping down, down across the grey-green slope. In a moment they were into the dip and lost to view. Perhaps it had been imagination . . . it had been such a quick glimpse after all. . . . No! there was another, in pink, and another and another. Three more, then a whole bunch of flying horsemen until the slope was thick with them. She could see it all. Some were jumping the fence below Marly church, more came riding between the big park trees.

She went to the window and listened, and then she heard the music of hounds, very faint and intermittent, and the long mournful shout of a Huntsman, like a man calling in cattle from the pastures. More horsemen coming down through the trees, and last, three figures, appearing very small like pygmies, running down after them.

Then Bumpus, tottering along the edge of the lawn, hat in hand, followed by the gardener's boy in a faded blue jersey. . . . She sat in the chair, frozen with an awful fear and excitement. . . .

THERE! the first hound breaking through the hedge, several more clambering over the fence . . . sounds of yelpings, loud now and continuous. . . . More and more hounds, all over the lawn now, feathering about among the withered hollyhock rods . . . more, bursting through the laurel bushes. One hound, stuck half-way through the fence, working its body frantically to get through. . . . There they go across the lawn into the bushes on the far side, and here comes the huntsman wearing the famous white collar. . . . More riders, skirting the lower lawn and jumping the fence by the ha! ha! wall.

Oh, poor, poor Rufus. . . . There's old Bumpus, talking to the Huntsman, pointing towards the stables with his floppy hat. A whole bunch of riders, their horses blowing from the steep hill of the valley, passing at an easy canter over the tangled meadow grass. . . . They must not get him . . . not Rufus . . . any other fox, but not Rufus. . . .

But the whole bustle and clamour of the Hunt passes before the windows of Wildwoods like a torrent, there is no arresting it, nothing can stop it now . . . not even human pity or mercy—Rufus must die, must die, must die. . . .

A single hound, far behind the others, clambering clumsily through the fence, came loping up the gravel path and disappeared round the angle of the house. . . . In the shrubberies, a blackbird scolding. . . . ZINK, ZINK, ZINK . . . the Hunt had passed and gone down into the mists towards Hieaway. . . .

Pamela, standing at the half-open window now, was like a statue.

That afternoon, the fourteenth of November, Rufus had been lying in Clint Hill spinney. The night before he had killed a rabbit on the Brixworth road, that had been maimed by a passing car and could not get away. He had taken it into a field and eaten his fill, burying the rest close to a manure heap. Then he had gone off to Clint Hill to sleep off the effects of his meal. He was aware of the hounds in good time, but not before the whipper-in marked him away from the east corner. His meal had long been digested and he was in good trim, even though he limped slightly from his maimed foot. He went first to the railway, crossed it, and ran into Cottesbrook Park. Here, in the spinney, he tried an earth he knew well and found it stopped so he turned, right for Blueberry, and with eight fields in hand, went into the thickets between the double mounds. There were two other foxes in Blueberry, but somehow or other hounds, when they came up, still held their original line, and when Rufus left the spinney they were on his heels only five fields away, and short fields at that.

Rufus ran to Robins' farm, and as no one was about, went into the yard and rolled in the manure heap. This was a dodge he had learnt in one of his previous runs, and it served to give him

18—WL

a breathing space. Hounds checked for five minutes at the foil. In that time he slipped away at an easy pace for Coldhangar and tried the earth under the rhododendrons. . . . But that too was stopped.

Still with a good lead, he made for Maidwell Dales, and the scuttering moor-hens told of his passage through the reeds. Skirting Penny Plain and the lane where he encountered the gipsies, he went across to Hopping Hill. Here he was seen by a roadmender and a passing motorist, who stopped to see the fun. He crossed the road and ran up the brook towards Draughton. He began to feel weary so he lay up in the reeds of a little field pond. He waited for such a long time that a water-rat came out of the bank and sat on a little platform of withered sedges, nibbling a green shoot. Rufus, muddied and tired, watched it through his cunning slits, one ear still upright like a shark's fin. After a while it slipped off into the water and a ring under the farther bank told Rufus the rat had gone to earth. Then followed an uneventful pause, in which rooks cawed sleepily and a distant train went puffing up the valley.

About ten yards away, in the red-berried hedge, was a tall dead tree, struck and riven by lightning one summer night long years ago. To this tree a wood-pigeon came and sat for a long while on a dead splinter, puffed out into a grey ball. Then it began to crane its neck about and finally launched itself into space and came to a clappering landing on the margin of the little pond about five feet from where Rufus lay, hidden in the reeds. It waddled down to the water, after a good look round, and plunged its beak right in, not sipping like other birds, but drinking greedily with submerged bill. After taking its fill, it sat a moment, rather puffily and with raised crest, then flew heavily back to the tree, where it started to preen. All the while Rufus watched it, but his ears were alert to catch the faintest sound of pursuit.

On the dead bough, the pigeon turned and fanned its tail, working its soft broad bill round the root. Then it lifted its left wing and preened vigorously until a tiny speck of blue fluff floated down and lit with a gentle kiss on the weedy water.

Far away a song-thrush started to sing. . . . "Puwee, Puwee, Puwee. . . . Chip-uuuu, Chip-uuuu, Chip-uuuu" . . . and the pure notes sounded like a fairy flute. Redwings passed over, and some, arresting their flight, dived down with closed wings on to the dead tree. Up the hedge Rufus saw a rabbit hopping along, among some very pale green crab apples. It squeezed through the hedge and vanished. And still Rufus did not stir. Something told him he was being followed. . . .

On the other side of the little pond, its massive girth hidden in a welter of red berries of hips and haws, was a splendid oak tree. In this sheltered hollow, the frosts had miraculously spared the leaves and the foliage was still thick, almost green near the base. The upper part of the tree had turned a lovely amber colour here and there, but it would be some weeks yet before all its leaves would fall. This tree seemed so splendidly sturdy and strong, so well grown and rich, and clusters of appetising acorns peeped from between the thick clumps of leaves. Over a generation it had grown in that spot, sown by a passing bird, dead now these many years. Season after season it had grown, pushing its way upwards through the tangling undergrowth, and much had happened in that time. In its early life the railway had come stealing up the valley, with the sound of shovels and picks at work, and later the first train, puffing and panting up the slope. Rooks were feeding on the acorns now, shaking the thick boughs as they feasted greedily, and several wood-pigeons had visited it in the early part of the afternoon.

The rooks were far too busy stuffing themselves to notice the advent of Rufus, and now he was lying well screened in the rusting reed spears by the water's edge. "Caw caw," said the rooks, and now and then an acorn would come tumbling down, some falling with a loud plop into the pond and sending widening rings shaking to the weeds. Soon an aeroplane passed over, very high, and droning like a bee. Up there a man was sitting in a frail cockpit, removed from this world below, where a tired fox lay panting by a little pond and blue-shot rooks were feeding on the acorns. He did not even see the moving specks of red and black coming up to the gorse. Almost a disembodied spirit, the pilot flew on towards the east.

One by one the rooks left the oak tree and flew away, until there were only five left. These soon all left together with many caws, and glided down on a stubble field, three meadows away, where some partridges were moving, like brown slugs, over the stubbly ochre spikes.

Rufus, lying still in the reeds, noted all these things, even the aeroplane. He watched the latter come into a small square of sky that showed between the reed spaces, and pass resolutely across, like a steady flying gnat—indeed, he thought it was one. And then the pigeon on the dead tree ceased to preen. It was drawing itself up, and no longer sat bunched up, with its pink toes hidden by soft fluff. A wood-pigeon has sharp eyes, and can see a long way, nearly a mile, and now it was watching something very intently, away on the other side of the line. Its body seemed to become thinner and thinner, and then with one last look, it left the dead bough and flew away. For a second or two the dead branch rocked to and fro—one two, one two, one two—and then became static.

Rufus heard the pigeon take wing from the dead branch, and the redwings flew upwards and away on enviable wings into the soft grey sky. He heard, above his pumping heart, the hounds speaking to his trail and the clatter of the cavalcade as they crossed the metals. So he slipped out of the reeds and went up the ditch by the crab apples. He squeezed through the same place as the rabbit, and followed its trail until he reached a bramble brake. Clinging to the spined thicket were some rose-red leaves, and long yellow grass grew up between the raking branches. Rufus turned aside here, and went up the slope of a little hill, where some sheep were grazing. He was heading now for Scaldwell Wood, but the long climb from the valley had winded him, and he was feeling the effects of his maimed paw. No longer did he slip along at an easy lope, and his tongue was hanging.

Five fields away the hounds came up the ditch past the little pond. They had smelt the spot where Rufus had lain, and they went yelling up the ditch, scattering the rusty leaves. From the bramble brake the rabbit rushed, pursued for some yards by one of the young entry, who got the crack of a whip lash in his ear to teach him not to riot. Then they took the line at a fast pace up the hill, checking a little when they came to the sheep.

Meanwhile, Rufus, tiring still, crossed the Draughton road into Lamport Park. And then he did a cunning thing. He first made a dead line for Scaldwell spinney, and when within a hundred yards, he back trailed for about fifty, and scrambled up into the oak tree where he used to kennel. It was not long before the sounds of pursuit came to his ears. The hounds appeared across the park, materialising like magic out of the shrubs and coming at a great pace across the withered winter sward. They swirled round the tree in a torrent and carried on for Scaldwell Wood. The Huntsman naturally thought he had gone there, though hounds began to falter a little on the outskirts of the spinney. Now the park was dotted with riders and a man dismounted close to the oak and tightened up the horse's girth. He could smell the sweaty horse and man beneath the tree. Then the man mounted again and walked slowly off to join some more riders that stood their restless mounts about fifty yards distant.

Rufus could hear the horn blowing its sad music in the wood, and hounds were now silent. He prayed that another fox might be there, but the spinney was deserted and hounds came filtering out of the rides, noses to ground, completely at fault. In a moment the hounds would be brought back and then the game would be up. Rufus took a furtive peep and saw the horsemen had their backs to him. They were talking, and one was smoking a cigarette, which showed he was not a good foxhunter. Rufus slipped down a sloping branch and dropped to the ground as light as an autumn leaf. He was half-way across the park and nearly into a holly plantation, when a boy, standing on the wall that bordered the park, saw him and gave the halloa!

Very soon he heard the hound voices again, speaking to his trail, and a leaden weight seemed to drag upon his feet. Straining for air, for more air, his back began to arch, and from his lolling pink tongue little drops of saliva dripped off into the grass, and flecked his muddied coat. Everywhere eyes seemed to mark his passage, and to point the way he had fled. The lodge keeper by the grey-lichened gates bearing their noble swans saw him crossing the park. He ran past the long, many-windowed house, with its family thoughts graven for ever on the weathered stone . . . "In things transitory resteth no Glory" . . . and the windows were aflame with sunset, yellow and vivid, shining through the autumn trees. He crossed the winding drive, brushing lightly through the amber leaves that lay in great drifts under the beeches, and chaffinches flew up to the lower branches, white-barred wings showing vividly. They sat and "pinked" at Rufus until he dived into the box bushes.

Hounds were gaining on him now, gaining, yes, gaining. . . . When he crossed the main road they were only a few hundred yards behind, and horsemen were already coming out of the lodge gates and galloping along the turf at the side of the road. The school-children were coming home and they saw Rufus cross. The air became shrill with their excited cries.

Below him the valley fell away to the brook and the yellow sunset was flashing in some flood water. Night was not so far distant, and already the pigeon hosts were streaming across to roost in Hieaway. Wearily Rufus turned along the ridge, and as he did so the last gleam of sunlight was shut out. There were a lot of bramblings and chaffinches feeding in the beech mast and they flew up in waves as he loped through them.

There stood Marly church; he could see it now, and the thick belt of trees that told of Wildwoods, and thither he ran, slower now and slower, so that the Huntsman viewed him. Down the valley now, where the going was easier, across the brook, where he stopped a moment to lap greedily and bathe his poor tired feet. Then on again up the gentle slope to the garden of Wildwoods. He saw the reek of a bonfire, and something made him turn for it; the pungent smoke might foil the hounds.

And that is where Pamela, watching from the long windows, saw him—a hunted, beaten fox at his last gasp. She did not know (how could she?) that it was the selfsame fox that she had rescued from starvation in Coldhangar so long ago. Had she known, the fluttering farewell of the lime tree leaves might have had a more subtle significance. . . .

He went past the stables, slipped, unseen by the busy chauffeur, into the kitchen garden, and down through the cabbages into the field. Six fields away was Hieaway, and there was an earth that offered sanctuary. . . . IF it was not stopped. But could he do it? It had been a seven-mile point and Rufus was almost done. Only a quarter of the field was up now, and the rest were jogging home. On! On! On! There had been a time before when those dark fir trees offered shelter and he had only just made it. But then he had to climb the hill; now it was on the same ridge.

Some cattle came blowing after him and actually stamped round him with tossing heads and rolling eyes. The smell of them might have checked the hounds, but he was viewed by the Huntsmen, and was as good as lost. He MUST make Hieaway . . . he MUST.

Four fields . . . three fields . . . two, one . . . and he was still ahead of the leading hound, though not twenty yards separated them in the last burst.

Rufus, his hard life and training standing him in good stead, made one final burst of speed. If this failed he was lost. His brush was raised and his back no longer arched; it was the last great effort. He gained the hedge with the jaws of Orator not a foot behind, and once through the binders of the thorns the hound was at a disadvantage. The lissom little prey could slip in between the thick underbrush. Rufus dragged himself up to the earth. It was open . . . the earth where he had been born.

He went down, slowly.

The little pine-needled hill was alive with hounds and men. Under the dark firs and sombre shadows the pink coats sang out in vivid spots of colour, and the white breeches of the dismounted men were the most vivid spots of all. A woodman in leather apron and a bill-hook in his hand came up over the mound.

"Aye, I seed 'im goo to groun' unner this 'ere tree, I reckon 'e's the one-eared ole fox that's been plaguing us for weeks past."

The Huntsman frowned. He would have liked to have left Rufus in peace, but like Pilate, he had to respect the people. If he was to leave this fox, the Hunt would get a bad name for letting them go free and that would mean foxes being shot. And yet . . . there was only a little time left, folly to start digging now. But hedge caffender was anxious and pleading, so the terrier was sent for, a sturdy little beast with a black saddle, and the pluck of Rufus himself.

The second whipper-in came up through the darkling trees with a couple of spades, and the terrier was pushed into the hole. He went down, excitedly, scrabbling the red earth. The second whipper-in lay with his ear to the ground, listening, but he could hear nothing. There was a hushed silence then, and the dark trees seemed to shut out most of the lingering light.

From the wood, riders began to move slowly away, talking and chattering excitedly, for it had been a great run. But a few still remained; some dismounted and stood by their tired horses.

All the birds in Hieaway were very silent, not a robin piped nor a wren scolded. Gravely watching the scene through half-closed eyes was the old owl in his big tree, who had first seen Rufus as a wee cub, playing with fir-cones on the sandy bank.

Soon there was a rushing noise and a great cloud of wood-pigeons circled round. But they were afraid to come in

He went down slowly

to roost for they saw the floor of the wood alive with hounds and men. Some of the hounds sat down on their haunches, watching the earth, others wandered about the wood looking rather bored.

At the foot of the great pine sprawled the whipper-in. He had taken off his velvet hunting cap and his hair was wet with sweat. Now there was a muffled yapping deep below under the pine, and the sound of battle, thumps and snarls. In a short while the terrier came out slowly backwards, his stump of a tail tight between his legs and his face bloody. In vain did the whipper-in urge him to enter the earth again; for the first and last time in his life the terrier had met his match.

Then the men started to dig. The whipper-in took off his coat and the woodman did likewise, and they toiled under the pine root. Slowly it got darker and the last horseman trotted away from the wood.

"Well, try and get him out," said the Huntsman. "It's my belief you'll find him dead. I think the terrier has killed him."

The whipper-in shook his head. "I don't think so; look at his tail. I've never known him to put his tail down when he's killed a fox."

"Well, do your best. You can't have much further to dig."

The men went on digging until a great scar was cut across the root of the tree, and the whipper-in was almost hidden by the mound of red soil.

The Huntsman called the disappointed hounds, and they trailed away, one by one, into the shadows. Only the terrier remained, hind legs shivering, and growling quietly at unpleasant memories. Though he tried now and again to help the toiling man, he would not venture down into the hole.

Down by the gate a horse whinnied for the whipper-in, and champed grass between clinking bit. Carrion crows, like a cloud of evil spirits, circled the wood, cawing hoarsely, for they dared not come in to roost.

"Phew, I sweat!" The hedge caffender passed his brown knotted hand across his forehead and clumsily came out of the excavation. "You 'ave a goo, mate. We'll 'ave 'im afore long, 'e can't be much furder in, the b——r." But the spade gashed a great root and made a scar like blood upon it, so fierce had been the blow. "Ah, that's why the tarrier couldn't get at 'im proper . . . we'll never get 'im outer this now."

And sure enough, the mighty pine root was like a great hawser, barring the way to the digging men. The whipper-in tossed the spade out of the hole and it slithered a little way down the sand. He reached for his coat and put it on. He tried to brush some or the soil from his white breeches, for they were a sorry sight and would take hours to clean.

"Reckon we'll 'ave to let him be; Corfield'll catch it from the Master for this, 'e was told to stop this earth. . . . Anyway, 'e was a game 'un." . . . They went off down the bank.

Now the carrions began to circle the wood again, cawing, cawing in the quiet. Then they all came in to roost, clumsily flapping in the topmost oak branches. Some low-flying pigeons came and went straight into the tangled shadow of the pine tops.

The wood had been raped of its peace and it would take some time to recover. In the burries and under the brambles the rabbits still cowered; birds were watchful in the thick bushes.

A lovely silence fell upon this sombre place. The huge pine stood, with the fresh scarred earth at its root, and the signs of ugly man all about. Hound droppings soiled the rusty leaves, and there was a torn Woodbine packet under the hollies. What a peace, this, after the bustle and turmoil of the last few hours!

The old owl flitted from his hollow tree and glided away, and a minute later his quavering cry floated up to the mound.

In the tops of the pines the night wind was crooning so softly

—"Rush, rush, rush"—as though it would lull all its pitiful little woodland people to a never-ending sleep.

The first stars began to wink over the valley and one peeped down through the crevices of the dark interlacing branches.

And still, in the Hieaway firs . . . that sleepy surf of sound.

It is quiet now in the kennels save for the whimper of a sleeping hound or the rustle of straw on the benches as a dream-ridden leg thrusts spasmodically.

It is quiet also in the stables and in the dwellings of mankind. Strange this stilling of movement, this closing of eyes! Magical slumber, magical silences!

Such a short while ago all these actors in the past drama were afire with movement and life.

Where now the blackbirds that ran upon the lawn before the windows of Wildwoods, where the rooks, busy among the fruitful oak branches by the leaf-strewn pond?

Even the great cities are strangely muted and dimmed, the humming in the hive is low.

There is a waiting for the light, for the sun again. The birds and animals sleep as insects sleep in the chinks of a wintry tree, and even the astonishing brain of man comes under this magic spell, and reason yaws like a rudderless ship among the troubled seas of dreams.

The Huntsman sleeps, on his back and snoring; the whipper-in is busy with foxy phantoms, muttering to himself.

Buried deep within many walls the Master sleeps, and only a mouse is awake in his dressing-room, gnawing the woodwork under a wardrobe.

Old Bumpus, in flannel night-shirt, is playing a steady solo on the nosoon, an alarm clock to keep him monotonous company.

Under the cold sky and keen sweet airs the dark hump of

Hieaway is still breathing; it seems that even the trees are dreaming.

Yet there is one that sleepeth not.

See! a shadow comes stealing from the skirts of the firs and goes, noiselessly, down into the valley fields, limping slightly with the old limp, one ear erect like a shark's fin.

May the good earth keep you, now and for always! Good hunting, little red fox, and . . . good-bye!

THE END